Geography 21
BOOK 1

THE UNITED KINGDOM

www.C̶ᴜ̶
On-line support

© HarperCollinsPublishers L   ᴜᴜᴜ

First published 1999
Reprinted 1999, 2000
ISBN 000 326694 X

Simon Ross asserts the moral right to be identified as the author of this work.

British Library Cataloguing in Publication Data
A catalogue record for this book is available from the British Library.

Project management by Anne Montefiore
Edited by Susan Millership
Cover design by Derek Lee
Internal design by Glynis Edwards
Index by Kay Wright
Illustrations by Barking Dog Art, Jerry Fowler and Jeremy Gower
Production by Anna Pauletti
Printed and bound by Printing Express, Hong Kong

Dedication

To the pupils of Berkhamsted Collegiate School for their inspiration and a special thanks to my wife, Nikki, and children, Susannah and James

Acknowledgements

Richard Young and Philip Durham of Photoair
JA Dingle of Looe Library
Peter Smith Photography
Mark Goddard of British Geological Survey
Carl Michalski of New Forest District Council
Ken Gardner of Landform Slides
MF Davies and Jan Williams of the Environment Agency
Bob and Mary Walters
Pat Webb
Sue Locke of British Cement Association
Charles Eaton
Dr Olly Watts of the RSBP
Dr David Hilling
David Miller, Reserve Manager, Beinn Eighe and Loch Maree Islands NNRS
Maps reproduced from Ordnance Survey mapping with the permission of the Controller of Her Majesty's Stationery Office © Crown copyright; Licence Number 433772.

Photographs and Maps
Action Plus: 87l /Steve Bardens
Adur District Council: 78t
Blue Circle: 68 t and c
Bowmans Farm: 12r
British Geological Survey, reproduced by permission of the Director, ©NERC. All rights reserved: 55
Christie's Images: 70b
City Repro / The City of Newcastle upon Tyne: 39bl, 42
Alison Doggett: 12l
Eldon Square Associates Ltd: 39l
Garden and Wildlife Matters: 7r, 30t
Geo Science Features: 57t, 88, 95
Robert Harding: 7t /Raj Kamal, 71 / Kathy Collins, 7c /Roy Rainford, 33t /Lee Frost, 43t and 46 /Philip Craven, 56 /Adam Woolfitt, 62tl, 62tr /Don Williams, 66l /Richard Ashworth, 66r /Ian Griffiths, 73t / Duncan Maxwell
Hampshire Waste Services Limited / Jon Banfield: 78br, 79l
Lifelife: 62br /David Thompson
Mercury Press Agency: 43b
NASA: 6t and c

Newcastle City Council / ESR Cartography: 40
Newcastle United Football Company Limited: 39r
Nexus: 39br, 41
Ordnance Survey © Crown copyright: 15, 16, 17, 23, 27, 28, 37, 38, 59, 91
Original Organics Limited.: 79r
Papilio Natural History and Travel Library: 87r /Robert Pickett
The Post Office: 70t and c
Photoair: 14b, 31, 34b, 59t
Simon Ross: 11cr, 33, 35l, 52b, 59b, 78bl, 81bc, 94
RSPCA: 47t/Tony Sutch, 47b/Jonathan Plant
Science Photo Library: 6bl and r, 47
Scottish Highland Photo Library: 90br
Scottish Natural Heritage: 84t, 90bl, 91t
Andrew Sole: 35tr
Tony Stone Images: 62bl /Chris Bessell, 81cl /Mike Caldwell
Vauxhall Motors Limited: 61, 64
Woodfall Wildlife Images: 52t, 67, 73t and 77t, 82t, 84b, 93 /David Woodfall, 54 /Adrian Dorst, 89 / Peter Wilson

Geography 21
BOOK 1

THE UNITED KINGDOM

Simon Ross
Head of Geography, Berkhamsted Collegiate School

Series Consultant: Michael Raw
Head of Geography, Bradford Grammar School

Collins Educational
An Imprint of HarperCollins*Publishers*

CONTENTS

Locations featured

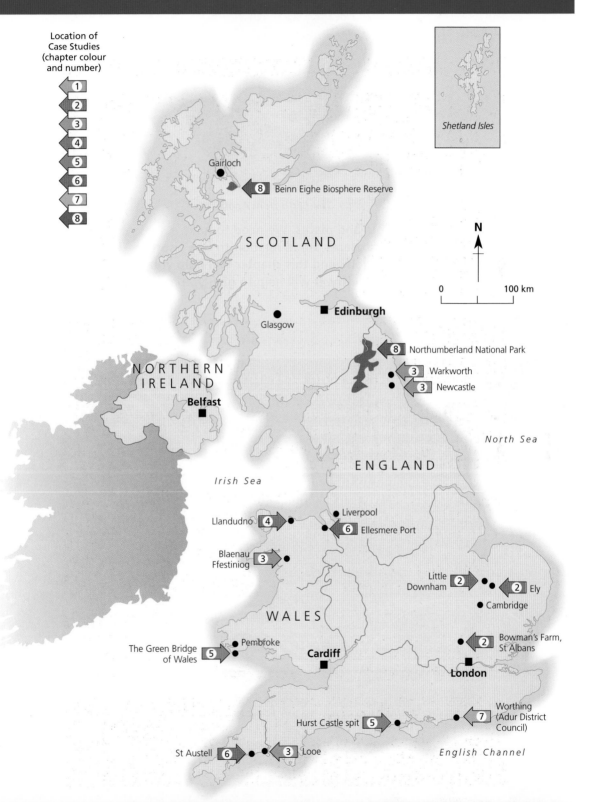

Location of Case Studies (chapter colour and number)

1
2
3
4
5
6
7
8

Shetland Isles

SCOTLAND

Gairloch

8 Beinn Eighe Biosphere Reserve

N

0   100 km

Glasgow

■ Edinburgh

8 Northumberland National Park

3 Warkworth

3 Newcastle

NORTHERN IRELAND

■ Belfast

North Sea

ENGLAND

Irish Sea

Liverpool

Llandudno 4

6 Ellesmere Port

Blaenau Ffestiniog 3

Little Downham 2

2 Ely

Cambridge

WALES

Cardiff ■

2 Bowman's Farm, St Albans

The Green Bridge of Wales 5

Pembroke

London ■

Worthing (Adur District Council) 7

Hurst Castle spit 5

St Austell 6

3 Looe

English Channel

A sense of place

▲ *1.1 The Earth from Apollo 11*

Geography is about people and places. We need to have a sense of place so that we can understand where places are in relation to one another. This book is all about the United Kingdom, and this chapter will help you learn the basic geography of our country. It will help to give you a sense of place.

1 Seeing from a distance

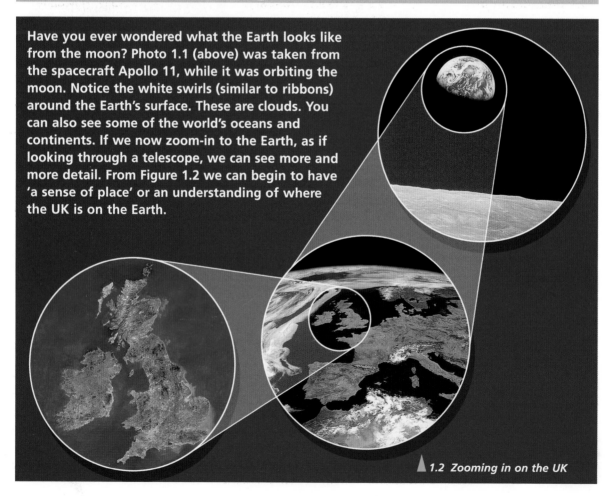

Have you ever wondered what the Earth looks like from the moon? Photo 1.1 (above) was taken from the spacecraft Apollo 11, while it was orbiting the moon. Notice the white swirls (similar to ribbons) around the Earth's surface. These are clouds. You can also see some of the world's oceans and continents. If we now zoom-in to the Earth, as if looking through a telescope, we can see more and more detail. From Figure 1.2 we can begin to have 'a sense of place' or an understanding of where the UK is on the Earth.

▲ *1.2 Zooming in on the UK*

Look at Photos 1.3 – 1.6 to see a range of **landscapes** found in the UK. In Books 2 and 3, we will zoom-out from the UK to study many other aspects of the geography of our planet.

1.3 Bull Ring Centre, Birmingham ▶

▲ *1.4 Glencoe, Scotland*

▲ *1.5 The Giant's Causeway, Northern Ireland*

▲ *1.6 Avon Valley, Hampshire*

A sense of place in the UK

Do you know the difference between the United Kingdom and Great Britain? And what exactly are the British Isles? It is very important that you understand these differences and that you use the correct terms:

- **British Isles** = all of the United Kingdom and the Republic of Ireland
- **Great Britain** (sometimes called Britain) = England, Wales and Scotland
- **United Kingdom** = England, Wales, Scotland and Northern Ireland.

> **1** Look at maps a, b and c on Figure 1.7. Work out which one shows:
> - the British Isles
> - Great Britain
> - the United Kingdom.

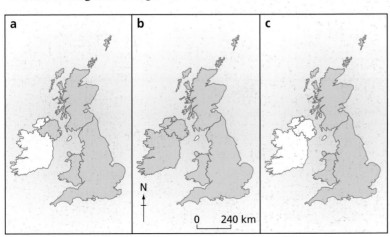

a b c

0   240 km

◀ *1.7*

In this book you will be studying the places marked on the location map on page 5. But before you start you will need to check your basic geography of the UK. The following activities review the locations and names of the major cities, rivers and uplands of the UK.

Before you start this activity make sure you have a large outline map of the UK. Remember to mark things in pencil before using colours and ink.

2 Look at Atlas Map A, opposite, and Figure 1.8 to help you with the following tasks. On your outline map of the UK:

a Shade and label the upland areas.

b Draw and label the Rivers Thames, Trent, and Severn.

c Draw and label the Rivers Tees, Tyne, Clyde and Tamar.

d Draw and label Lough Neagh in Northern Ireland.

e Name these islands:
- Isle of Wight
- Anglesey
- Isle of Man
- Outer Hebrides
- Shetland Islands.

f Name these sea areas:
- English Channel
- Atlantic Ocean
- Irish Sea
- North Sea.

g Use Atlas Map B, page 10, to help you label:
- England
- Wales
- Scotland
- Northern Ireland
- Republic of Ireland.

h Mark the cities on Figure 1.8 on your map (the first letter of each one is on the figure). Use Atlas Map B, page 10, to name them correctly.

Make sure your map has a title, key, north point and a scale.

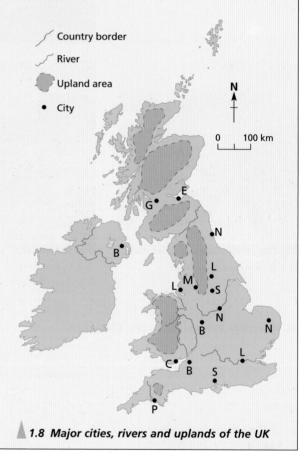

Key:
- Country border
- River
- Upland area
- • City

0   100 km

1.8 Major cities, rivers and uplands of the UK

3 **Relief** is the physical landscape of an area. It describes the lie of the land – the mountains and the lowland. Look carefully at Atlas Map A, opposite, and answer the following:

a What is the name of the highest mountain in the UK?
- How high is it above sea level?
- In which upland area is this mountain found?

b What is the name of the highest mountain in Wales?
- How high is it above sea level?
- In which upland area is it found?

c What is the name of the highest mountain in England?
- How high is it above sea level?
- In which upland area is it found?

d What is the name of the highest mountain in Northern Ireland?
- How high is it above sea level?

e What is the name of the highest point on Dartmoor?
- How high is it above sea level?

f Which range of hills lies between the Rivers Thames and Severn?

g Name two moors in South West England.

h Name the three rivers that form the edge of the North York Moors.

i Name the flat and low area of land in East Anglia that lies between the Rivers Wensum and Waveney.

j Where are the Antrim Mountains?

ATLANTIC OCEAN

North Sea

Irish Sea

Celtic Sea

English Channel

Atlas Map A

Orkney Islands
Mainland
Hoy
Pentland Firth
Duncansby Head

Cape Wrath
Butt of Lewis

Shetland Islands
Yell
Foula
Mainland
Fair Isle
Sumburgh Head
60°N
58°N

St Kilda

Outer Hebrides
Lewis
Clisham 799
Harris
North Uist
Skye
South Uist
Barra
Rum
Coll
Tiree
Mull
Ben More 966
Firth of Lorn
Jura
Islay

The Minch
Loch Broom
Dornoch Firth
Moray Firth

North West Highlands
Loch Ness
Ben Nevis 1344
Cairngorm Mts
Spey
Dee
Ben Macdhui 1309
Don

Grampian Mts
Ben Lawers 1214
Loch Tay
Tay
Firth of Tay
Ochil Hills
Loch Awe
Loch Lomond
Forth
Firth of Forth
Inner Hebrides

Arran
Firth of Clyde
Clyde

Southern Uplands
Merrick 843
Tweed
Cheviot Hills
Tyne

Malin Head
Erngal 752
Foyle
Bann
Antrim Mts
Lough Neagh
Lagan
North Channel

Donegal Bay
Lower Lough Erne
Upper Lough Erne
Shannon
Erne
Mourne Mts
Slieve Donard 852
Dundalk Bay
Boyne

Lough Conn
Achill
Lough Mask
Lough Corrib
Lough Ree
Lough Derg
Galway Bay
Shannon
Barrow
Suir
Blackwater
Carrantuohill 1041
Cape Clear
angle B.

Isle of Man
Solway Firth
Scafell Pike 977
Lake District
Morecambe Bay
Ribble
The Pennines
Tees
North York Moors
Ouse
Derwent
Flamborough Head
Spurn Head
Mouth of the Humber

Liffey
Lughaquilla Mtn 926
Wicklow Mts

Anglesey
Caernarfon Bay
Snowdon 1085
Dee
Mersey
High Peak
Kinder Scout 636
Trent
The Wash
Wensum
Norfolk Broads
Waveney

Cardigan Bay
Cambrian Mountains
Teifi
Severn
Great Ouse
The Fens

St George's Channel
St David's Head
Wye
Severn
Avon
Cotswold Hills
Chiltern Hills
Thames

Carmarthen Bay
Black Mountains
886 Breacon Beacons
Severn
Avon
Thames
North Downs

Bristol Channel
Exmoor
Mendip Hills
Salisbury Plain
South Downs
Dungeness
Beachy Head

Bodmin Moor
Dartmoor Yes Tor 619
Tamar
Exe
Lyme Bay
Bill of Portland
New Forest
Isle of Wight

Isles of Scilly
Land's End
Lizard Point

Legend
over 1000 m
500 – 1000 m
200 – 500 m
100 – 200 m
0 – 100 m
land below sea level
1344 ▲ Mountain height (height in metres)
Scale 1 : 4 000 000
0   50   100   150 km

N

ATLANTIC

OCEAN

Stromness
Kirkwall
Thurso
Wick

Stornaway

Tarbert
Uig
Lochmaddy
Portree
Lochboisdale

Ullapool

Inverness

Aberdeen

North

Sea

Fort William

SCOTLAND

Tobermory
Oban

Dundee
Perth

Stirling

Glasgow
Ardrossan
Brodick
Ayr

Edinburgh
Berwick-upon-Tweed

Coleraine
Londonderry
Cairnryan
Larne
Donegal
Stranraer
NORTHERN
Enniskillen
IRELAND
Belfast
Lisburn

Dumfries
Morpeth
Newcastle-
upon-Tyne
Sunderland
Carlisle
Durham
Workington
Darlington
Middlesbrough

Scarborough

Ballina
Sligo
Newry
Dundalk
Drogheda

Douglas

Heysham
Lancaster
Harrogate
York
Kingston-upon-Hull
Fleetwood
Bradford
Blackpool
Preston
Blackburn
Leeds
Huddersfield
Doncaster
Grimsby
Bolton
Manchester
Sheffield
Lincoln
Liverpool
Stockport

Westport

REPUBLIC
OF
IRELAND

Dublin

Galway

Wicklow

Holyhead
Chester
Crewe
Stoke-on-
Trent
Derby
Nottingham
Kings
Lynn
Norwich
Caernarfon
ENGLAND
Leicester
Peterborough

Limerick

Shrewsbury
Telford
Wolverhampton
Coventry
Cambridge
Ipswich
Birmingham
Warwick
Northampton
WALES
Aberystwyth

Tralee

Wexford
Rosslare

Hereford
Luton
Harwich
Gloucester
Oxford
Watford
Cork

Waterford

Fishguard
Newport
Swindon
Slough
London
Southend-
on-Sea
Pembroke
Swansea
Bridgend
Cardiff
Bristol
Reading
Croydon
Sheerness
Ramsg
Bath
Ashford
Dover
Crawley
Folkestone

Taunton
Salisbury
Brighton
Hastings
Southampton
Eastbourne
Bournemouth
Portsmouth
Newhaven
Exeter
Poole
Weymouth
Torquay

Plymouth

Penzance
St Marys

English Channel

Irish
Sea

Atlas Map B

FRANC

Shetland
Islands
Lerwick

Legend:
- Country boundary
- Internal boundary
- Road
- Railway
- ✈ Airport
- ■ Capital city
- ● Main town or city
- ○ Other town or city

Scale 1 : 4 000 000

0   50   100   150 km

4 Fill in the missing letters to discover the names of the following cities in the UK. Use Atlas Map B to help you.

C _ r d _ _ f   _ e _ f _ s t
Ca _ b _ i _ g _   L _ v _ r _ _ o _
_ l _ s _ o w   Y _ _ k
B _ _ s t _ _   L _ e _ s
N _ t _ _ n _ h _ m   _ i _ d l _ s b r _ _ g _

5 Look at Table 1.9. Plot the location of the football teams on an outline map of the UK. Remember that some major cities have more than one team. You could use the team colours to make your map more attractive.

Arsenal	Coventry
Manchester United	Liverpool
Newcastle	Middlesbrough
Leeds	Aston Villa
Derby	Southampton
Chelsea	West Ham
Wimbledon	Leicester
Sheffield Wednesday	Blackburn
Tottenham	Everton
Charlton Athletic	Nottingham Forest

▲ *1.9 Football teams in the Premier League, 1998/9 season*

6 Table 1.10 lists the six longest rivers in the UK. This information can be shown in the form of a diagram (see Figure 1.11).

a Copy and complete the diagram in Figure 1.11, using information from Table 1.10.

b Use Atlas Map A, page 9, to plot the courses of the six rivers on an outline map of the British Isles.

River	Country	Length (km)
Severn	Wales + England	354
Thames	England	346
Tay	Scotland	188
Clyde	Scotland	158
Tweed	Scotland	155
Bann	Northern Ireland	122

▲ *1.10 The location and length of the longest rivers in the UK*

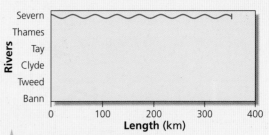

▲ *1.11 The six longest rivers in the UK*

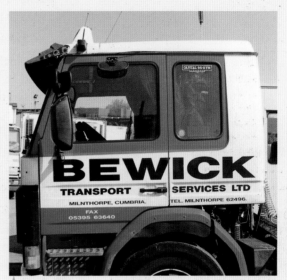

▲ *1.12 A lorry cab displaying the name of its base town*

7 Look at Photo 1.12. Notice that the town where the lorry is based is written on the side of the cab.

a Work in pairs, or as a class. Make a list of places written on lorries that travel along roads close to your school or home. (Be careful to stand well back from the road while conducting your survey.) You could also look at lorries in car parks or at motorway service stations.

b Use your own atlas or Atlas Map B, to locate these places on an outline map of the UK.

c Locate your home town or the place where you did your survey.

d Write a few sentences describing your map:
- What do you notice about the distribution of the lorry bases?
- Are they mostly clustered around your home town?
- Do they spread out along major roads and motorways?

11

OS mapwork

There are many different sorts of maps including sketch maps, atlas maps and the very accurate and detailed maps produced by the Ordnance Survey. Maps tell us where places are, and they can also be used to describe the landscape of an area.

1 Finding our way around

▲ 1.1 Bowman's Farm

▶ 1.2 Visitors' map for Bowman's Farm

Photo 1.1 shows people visiting Bowman's Farm near St Albans in Hertfordshire. Like several farms, it is open to the public to provide extra money for the farmer. The map in Figure 1.2 is given to all visitors to help them find their way around. It shows them where the different attractions are located. It also helps prevent visitors from wandering into private or dangerous areas of the farm.

1 Look at Figure 1.2.

a Where does the farm trail start?

b Which paddock would you visit immediately after being pecked by the chickens in the Pets Corner?

c What attraction is found opposite the Pigs & Piglets?

d What do you walk up to see the cows being milked?

e What is stored near the tractor shed?

f Where are the toilets located?

g You have just been bitten by a savage rabbit! Where can you get First Aid?

Different types of maps

Maps, like the one in Figure 1.2 are very common. You can find them mounted on walls in shopping centres or in newspapers alongside adverts (see Figure 1.3). They are often given out free at tourist sites.

One problem with a **sketch map** is that it is *not* drawn to **scale** (see Skills Box 1, page 14). This means that you do not know exactly how far one feature is from another.

To draw a map to scale takes a great deal of time and care. Nowadays professional map-makers use modern and expensive equipment such as satellites, high above the surface of the Earth, to ensure that maps are accurate. In England, Scotland and Wales, the most widely-used maps are produced by the Ordnance Survey. We call these **OS maps**.

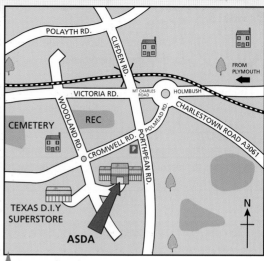

1.3 A sketch map

OS maps are drawn at a variety of scales:

- **Small-scale** maps cover large areas but do not give much local detail. Maps in atlases are good examples of small-scale maps

- **Large-scale** maps cover much smaller areas but give a lot more detail. Town maps that show road layouts are examples of large-scale maps.

The two most commonly used OS maps are the **1:50 000** maps and the **1:25 000** maps (see Figure 1.4). The following units in this chapter will help you to understand and use these maps.

---

2 Figure 1.3 shows a sketch map. As a class, find maps and plans for your local area. You could look through your local newspaper or visit libraries, shops and council offices (advertising/information leaflets often contain sketch maps).

3 Imagine that your class is to hold a summer fair in aid of a local charity. Here are some of the stalls and activities planned:
- **stalls** – tombola, plant, second-hand book, refreshment, cake
- **activities** – 'smash the plates', beat the goalie, basketball/netball, chip a golf ball into a bucket , throw ping-pong balls into jars, lucky dip.

a As a class suggest a few more stalls and activities.

b Identify where your school can hold the fair (playground, school fields?).

c Draw a sketch map on a large sheet of paper of the area that will be used for the fair.

d Suggest a layout for the fair. Remember that some things are more active than others and will need more room.

e Complete your sketch map by adding helpful information such as the location of the toilets and where cars may park.

4 Imagine that you are going to have a birthday party where you live. Draw a sketch map of your home area to help your friends find the party. Locate features such as roads, large trees, post boxes and shops to help your friends find their way.

1:25 000
large scale

a lot of local detail

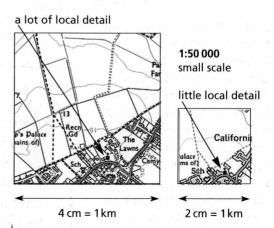

1:50 000
small scale

little local detail

4 cm = 1km   2 cm = 1km

1.4 Comparing small- and large-scale OS maps

SKILLS BOX 1

Scale

A **scale** is used to show how distances on a map differ from the way they are on the ground.

Linear scale

Kilometres

0   1   2   3   4   5

A ruler or paper edge marked with centimetre widths can be placed on the map to discover the distance on the ground in kilometres (see Skills Box 4, page 20).

Ratio scale

1:50 000 means that one centimetre on the map represents 50 000 centimetres (500 m) on the ground.

Therefore, on a 1:50 000 map, 2 cm represents 1 km on the ground.

On a 1:25 000 map, 4 cm represents 1 km on the ground.

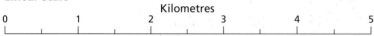

2 Map study: Ely (1:50 000)

Ely is a small cathedral city about 25 kilometres north of Cambridge (see Figure 2.1). Photo 2.2 is an **aerial** view of Ely. Can you see the Cathedral in the centre of the city? Now, find the Cathedral on the map in Figure 2.3. (You need to search for the letters *Cath*.)

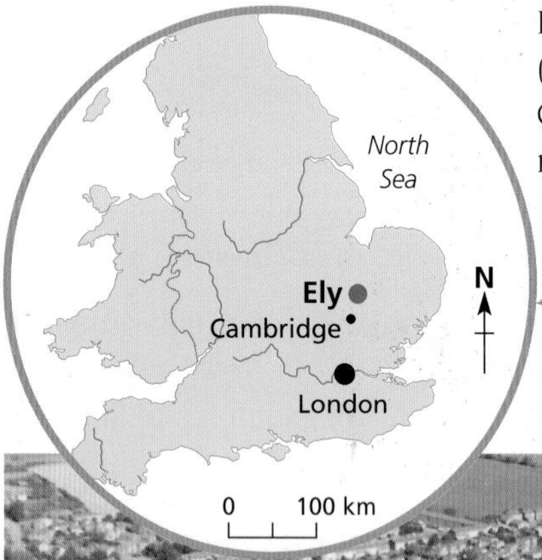

North Sea

Ely
Cambridge
London

N

0   100 km

2.1 Location of Ely, Cambridgeshire

2.2 Aerial view of Ely

D   C

A   B

Look again at Photo 2.2. All the detail that you can see – the houses, churches, roads, and open spaces – are also shown on the map in Figure 2.3. The map gives a bird's eye view of the landscape.

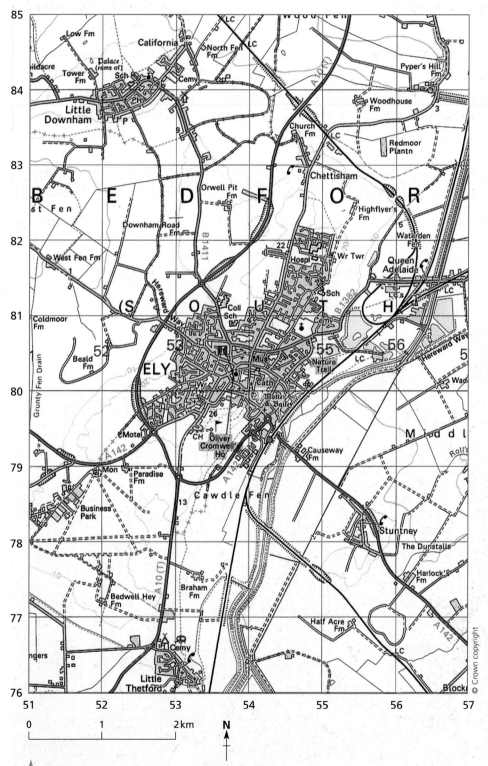

▲ *2.3 Ely and surrounding area, extract from 1:50 000 OS map (see Figure 2.4 for key)*

Map symbols

There is a great deal of information on most maps and not much space for labels. For this reason **symbols** are used to show features. (You saw symbols for toilets and First Aid on Figure 1.2, page 12.) Symbols are used all around us – road and parking signs are everyday examples.

Look at the key in Figure 2.4 on pages 16 and 17. There are a great number of symbols that can be used on a 1:50 000 map. You do not need to learn them all but you should know the basic ones. As you use maps more, you'll find that you recognise most of the symbols, and reading a map will become easier.

1 Take part in a Symbols Quiz by following these steps:

a Choose five OS map symbols and draw each one (very large) on a sheet of A4 paper.

b Fold your five pieces of paper and put them into a container that is passed around the class. (The class now divides into teams of three or four.)

c Taking it in turns, each team picks a piece of paper from the container and gives the correct meaning of the symbol. If the team gets it wrong, another team may answer.

d A correct answer scores two points. The winning team is the one that scores the most points.

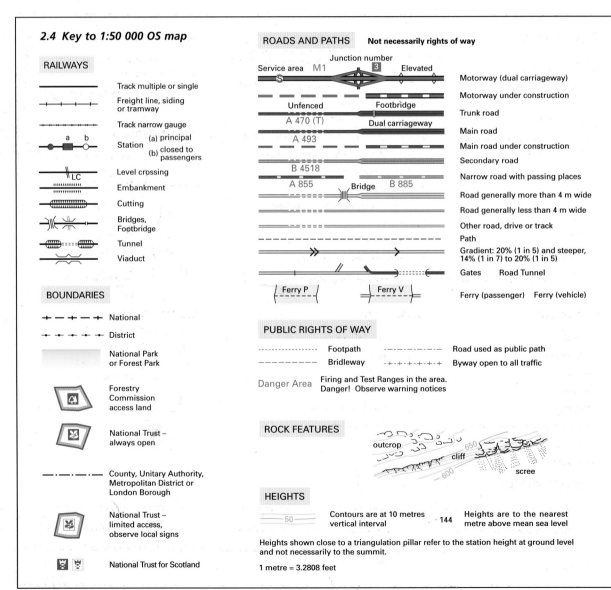

2.4 Key to 1:50 000 OS map

2 Look at Figure 2.5.

a Copy the symbols using the correct colours.

b Write alongside each symbol what it means. Use Figure 2.4 to help you.

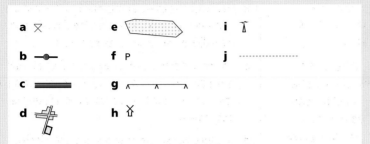

a ⋈   **e** ⬡   **i** ⋏

b ●—   **f** P   **j** ------------------

c ▬▬   **g** ⋏—⋏—⋏

d ✠   **h** ⋔

▲ **2.5 A selection of symbols used on 1:50 000 OS maps**

3 Use Figure 2.4 to help you draw the correct symbols for a:

- golf course
- railway embankment
- marsh or salting
- lighthouse (in use)
- quarry
- coniferous wood
- heliport
- milepost
- church with tower
- bus or coach station.

© Crown copyright

GENERAL FEATURES

 ruin Buildings

  Public buildings (selected)

  Quarry

Spoil heap, refuse tip or dump

Coniferous wood

Non-coniferous wood

Mixed wood

Orchard

Park or ornamental grounds

⋏—⋏—⋏ Electricity transmission line (with pylons spaced conventionally)

>--->---> Pipe line (arrow indicates direction of flow)

⋏ Radio or TV mast

Places of Worship { with tower / with spire, minaret or dome / without such additions }

○ Chimney or tower

Glasshouse

+ Graticule intersection at 5' intervals

Ⓗ Heliport

△ Triangulation pillar

⋔ Windmill with or without sails

Windpump/Wind generator

OTHER PUBLIC ACCESS

• • • Other route with public access

◆   ◆ National Trail, Long Distance Route, selected Recreational Paths

WATER FEATURES

Marsh or salting

Lake

Canal, lock and towpath

= = = = = = Canal (dry)

Aqueduct

Footbridge

Normal tidal limit

Lighthouse (in use and disused)

⚲ Beacon

Slopes

Cliff

Flat rock

Low water mark

High water mark

Sand

ABBREVIATIONS

P Post office
PH Public house
MS Milestone
MP Milepost
CH Clubhouse
PC Public convenience (in rural areas)
TH Town Hall, Guildhall or equivalent
CG Coastguard

ANTIQUITIES

+ Site of monument
• ○ Stone monument
VILLA Roman
Castle Non-Roman
⚔ Battlefield (with date)
☆ .... Visible earthwork

TOURIST INFORMATION

🄸 🄸 Information centre, all year/seasonal
▨ Selected places of tourist interest
🔆 Viewpoint
🅿 Parking

⋈ Picnic site
⋏ Camp site
🚐 Caravan site

▲ Youth hostel
⌐ Golf course or links
🚌 Bus or coach station

☎ Public telephone
☎ Motoring organisation telephone
PC Public convenience (in rural areas)

4 Look at Figure 2.6. Either on your own or in pairs:

a Decide what each symbol means.

b Think of some more everyday symbols and write them down or draw them

a

b

c

d

e

f

▲ *2.6 Symbols*

5 Study the map in Figure 2.3, page 15, and answer the following questions:

a What is the village in grid square 5578?

b Name the farm in grid square 5677.

c In which grid square are Ely Cathedral and Ely Museum?

d Give the four-figure reference for Pyper's Hill Farm.

6 Give the six-figure grid references for the following places:

a Camp site at Little Thetford

b Ely golf course

c Telephone at Chettisham

d Post Office in Little Downham

e Museum in Ely

f Church in Stuntney.

7 What is found at the following grid references:

a	525838	**d**	534763
b	550776	**e**	548792
c	568772	**f**	551834?

We make use of these gridlines to locate a grid square or a point on the map (see Skills Box 2, to discover how to use grid references).

Finding places

Gridlines

Finding places on maps is not always as easy as finding the cathedral in the centre of Ely. To locate somewhere quickly and accurately, we make use of the **gridlines** that criss-cross the map.

Look at Figure 2.3, page 15. Find the gridlines that run up and down the map. See how the numbers of these gridlines, written at the bottom of the map, increase in value from left (west) to right (east). These lines are called **eastings**. The gridlines that run across the map, with their values increasing from the bottom (south) to the top (north) are called **northings**.

Compass direction

Turn back to Photo 2.2 on page 14. Find the College shown by the letter C on the photo. Now look at the map in Figure 2.3 and locate the grid square 5381 (use Skills Box 2 to help). Can you find the College?

To describe where the College is in relation to the Cathedral we need to give a **compass direction** (see Skills Box 3). As north is 'straight up' on an OS map, we can say that the direction of the College from the Cathedral is roughly north-east.

Look back to Photo 2.2. Notice that the College lies in the distance, behind the Cathedral. By locating on the map the features that appear behind one another on a photo, we can say in which direction the photo is looking. We know from the map that the College is north-east of the Cathedral so the photo was taken looking north-eastwards.

SKILLS BOX 2 — Grid references

There are two important rules to remember:

1 The number written at the base of a gridline refers to the *next* square along.

2 The number from left to right across the map (**easting**) is always given first, *before* the number from bottom to top (**northing**). Remember, 'Along the corridor and up the stairs'.

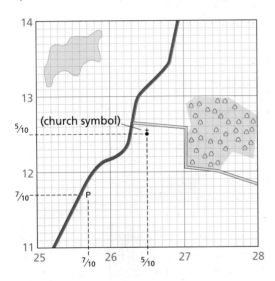

Four-figure references

A four-figure reference is used to locate a **grid square**. The trees in the map extract on the left are in grid square **2712**. (It is the square *after* the easting number 27 and *after* the northing number 12.) The grid reference for the lake is **2513**.

Six-figure references

A six-figure reference is used to locate a **point** on a map. For this you need to imagine that each grid square is divided into ten slices from top to bottom and from side to side.

Follow these steps to work out the six-figure reference for the church on the map on the left:

● Locate the church – as it lies between gridlines 26 and 27, the first two values will be **26.**

● The church lies five-tenths of the way between 26 and 27 so we add a 5 to the first two figures: **265** (this is the **easting** value and it makes up the first part of the reference).

● The church lies between the northing values 12 and 13 so the next two values are **12.**

● As the church is five-tenths of the way between 12 and 13 we add a 5 so the second group of numbers reads: **125** (this is the **northing** value).

● Now you put the easting and northing values together to get the final six-figure reference **265 125.**

Using the steps given, work out the six-figure reference for the Post Office on the map on the left.

SKILLS BOX 3 — Direction

The eight-points of the compass:

People give directions to describe where one place is in relation to another. For example, Leeds is north of Sheffield, or Sheffield is south of Leeds. However, you need to be careful when giving wind directions. This is because they are given as the direction that the wind has come from. For example, a north wind has come **from** the north.

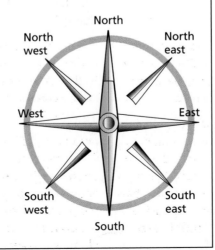

8 Use the compass points in Skills Box 3, to give the direction of the following places from Ely Cathedral on Figure 2.3, page 15:

a Ely Museum

b Hospital

c Golf course

d Railway station

e Tourist Information Centre.

The distance between places

Because an OS map is drawn to **scale** it is possible to work out the distance between two places. Find the College on the map in Figure 2.3 and locate the church with a spire at 538802. Place a ruler between the two places and measure the distance between them – you should find the distance is 2 cm. By measuring 2 cm on the linear scale, this represents 1 km on the ground. Therefore, we can now state that the College is 1 km to the north of the church.

Working out straight-line distance is quite easy. It is more complicated to work out distance along a curved route such as a road or a river (see Skills Box 4, to help you with this).

9 Look at Figure 2.3, page 15. A crow wants to fly in a straight line between the places given below. Work out the distance he will fly for each trip (you may need to use Skills Box 4, to help you).

a Ely Cathedral to Ely golf course.

b Ely Cathedral to Ely hospital.

c The Post Office in Little Downham to the camp site in Little Thetford.

d Half Acre Farm (554769) to Braham Farm (533775).

e Along the A10(T) from Little Thetford (527766) to the roundabout at 531788.

SKILLS BOX 4 — Distance

Straight-line distance

1 Use a ruler to measure the distance between two places on the map, in centimetres.

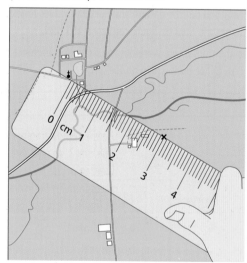

2 Measure out the distance on the map's linear scale to discover the distance on the ground in kilometres.

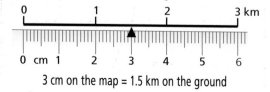

3 cm on the map = 1.5 km on the ground

Curved-line distance

1 Place the straight edge of a piece of paper along the route to be measured. Mark the start with the letter *S*. Look along the paper and mark off the point where the route moves away from the straight edge.

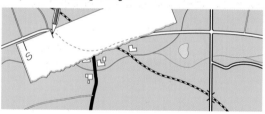

2 Pivot the paper and mark off the next straight section. Repeat this until you reach the end of the route. Mark this finishing point with the letter *F*.

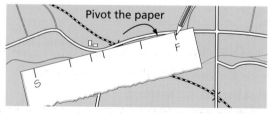

Pivot the paper

3 Place the edge of the marked paper alongside the linear scale on the map and convert the total length to kilometres.

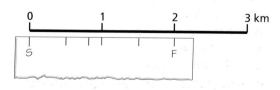

OS map work summary

10 Look at Photo 2.2 and Figure 2.3, pages 14 and 15.

a What colour (on the map) is the road marked A on the photo?

b Suggest what the land at B is used for.

c In which direction would you walk from B to the Cathedral?

d To the left of the Cathedral on the photo is a church with a spire. Draw the symbol for this type of church and find it on the map.

e What is the grid reference of the College (C)?

f What colour and number is the road marked D?

g Describe the open land to the south of the Cathedral.

h What do you think this land is used for?

11 Draw a sketch map to show some of the features on the map in Figure 2.3, page 15:

a Using a sharp pencil, draw a box to the same scale as the map extract (12 cm x 18 cm). Draw faint gridlines as they appear on the map. Write the numbers alongside the gridlines.

b Using Skills Box 5 to help you, plot the following features on to your sketch map:
- main roads (red on the map)
- secondary roads (brown on the map)
- railway lines
- the lakes near Ely
- Ely Cathedral
- rough outlines of the built-up areas of Ely, Little Downham, Stuntney and Little Thetford.

c Colour the features.

d Add a key, a north point and scale.

e Give your map a title: 'A sketch map of the Ely area'.

Drawing sketch maps from an OS map

There is a lot of detail on an OS map. Sometimes you may just want to look at specific details, and you can do this by drawing a **sketch map**. For example, you could just plot tourist attractions and main roads in an area.

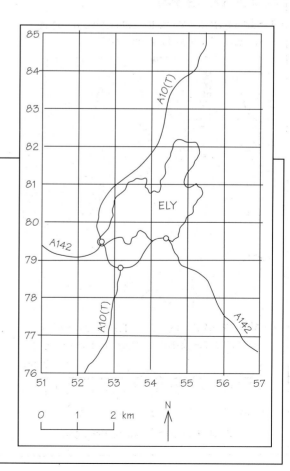

SKILLS BOX 5

How to draw a sketch map

1 Draw a grid with the same arrangement of squares as the map extract to be sketched. Reduce the grid squares for a reduction, or increase their size for an enlargement. The sketch map here is a **reduction**.

2 In pencil, draw on the features, using the gridlines to help you sketch accurately.

3 Complete your sketch by:
- adding colours
- numbering gridlines in ink
- giving the scale
- adding the north point
- writing names, any labels and a title for your map.

Figure 2.7 shows how a sketch map can be drawn to different scales. A sketch map can be drawn to the same scale as the OS map, reduced in size, or even enlarged (see Skills Box 5, page 21, for help on drawing sketch maps).

12 Look at Figure 2.3, page 15. Make an enlargement of grid square 5181 (see Skills Box 5, page 21 to help you).

a Draw a box 4 cm x 4 cm (4 cm = 1 km) which is double the size of the grid square on the map.

b Carefully plot the details shown in the grid square on to your map

c Complete your sketch by adding colours (if you wish), a key, a north point, a scale, and a title.

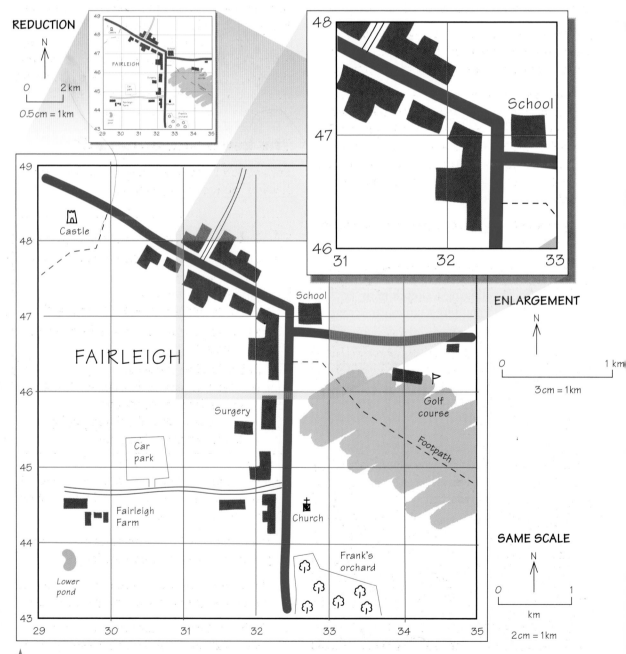

▲ *2.7 Sketch maps at different scales*

3 Looking at landscapes on maps

One of the most interesting things about an OS map is that it can tell us what the landscape looks like. We use the word **relief** to describe the ups and downs of a landscape.

Information on a map tells us whether it is an upland or a lowland area, and if the slopes are steep or gentle. It is possible to identify features of the landscape such as valleys, hills and cliffs.

Turn to the 1:50 000 OS map key in Figure 2.4, pages 16 and 17. Look for the heading HEIGHTS. Notice that heights are shown by two symbols:

- **Contours** are brown lines that are drawn at regular intervals to show heights above sea level. Contours join points of equal height. Look at the key to see at what interval the contours are drawn. You may need to follow a contour around the map until you find its height.

- **Spot heights** are used to give one-off heights above sea level.

On recent OS maps, all heights are given in metres. Notice in the key that heights are also given alongside a **triangulation pillar** (look up the symbol for

this feature). Triangulation pillars were used for surveying the land, but nowadays more up-to-date equipment is used, including satellites.

Contour patterns – what do they mean?

The pattern of contours on a map can tell us a lot about what the landscape looks like. Figure 3.2, page 24, shows some common contour patterns. Figure 3.3 is a **block diagram**, drawn from the contour information in Figure 3.2. Look carefully at the closeness of the contours. Can you see that the closer they are together, the steeper the slope? Look at how the contours form an upside-down 'V' shape where there is a river valley.

The landscape around Ely

Let's discover what the landscape is like in the Ely area. Start by doing Activity 1.

---

1 Look at the OS map of Ely in Figure 2.3 on page 15.

a Locate grid square 5280. There are two contours crossing this square.
- What are their heights?
- Which way is the land sloping in this square?

b Now locate grid square 5682. What is the spot height in this square?

c Look at the whole of Figure 2.3.
- What is the height of the *lowest* spot height? Give its six-figure grid reference.
- What is the height of the *highest* spot height? Give its six-figure grid reference.

After studying the contour patterns on Figure 2.3, we can now make the following statements about Ely and the land around it:

- The land is low lying, with much of it being less than 10 metres above sea level

- The contours are well spaced, suggesting that the land is quite flat with only gentle slopes

- The highest part of the map extract lies between 20 and 30 metres above sea level. This is where Ely has been built.

3.1 A triangulation pillar

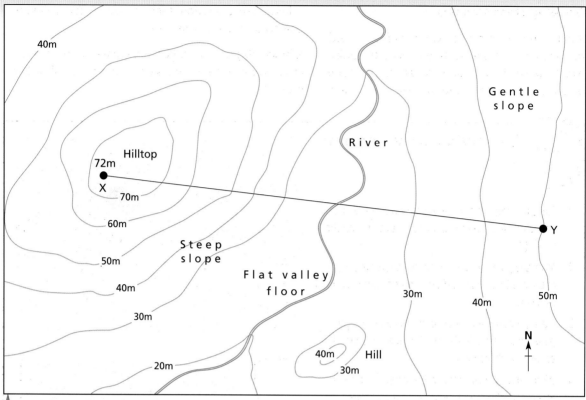

3.2 Relief features shown by contours on a map

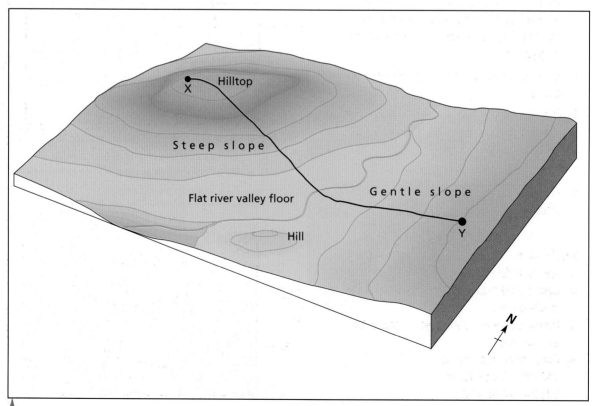

3.3 A block diagram of landscape shown in Figure 3.1

Drawing cross-sections

When you look at a map, you may find it hard to imagine what the landscape actually looks like. However, it is possible to use the contours on a map to create a sideways view of an area called a **cross-section**. (See to Skills Box 6, to learn how to draw a cross-section.)

A block diagram is similar to a cross-section but it gives you a better impression of an area by showing it in 3-D.

SKILLS BOX 6 — Drawing cross-sections

1 Place the edge of a piece of paper along the line of section. Mark on the paper the start (X) and the finish (Y).

2 Mark the points where the contours cross the paper and write their heights. Mark other features, such as rivers.

3 Place your marked paper on to a sheet of graph paper and draw a horizontal line the same length as the line of section (X-Y).

4 Work out a vertical scale. In this case, if you used an accurate scale (the same as the linear scale) your cross-section would be too flat to show the features of the landscape. Experiment with different scales – choose one that shows the features of the landscape clearly but is not too exaggerated.

5 Mark the contour values on the graph paper with crosses.

6 Join the crosses with a freehand line and continue to the edges of the graph. Notice how hilltops and valleys are curved.

7 Add labels to describe the features.

8 Complete your section by writing a title. Shade the section if you wish.

Helpful hints
- Always work in pencil – it's easy to make mistakes
- Double-check your contour values to make sure they're correct
- If contours are very close together, only mark alternate ones
- Good vertical scales to use:
  1:50 000 → 1 cm = 100 m
  1:25 000 → 1 cm = 20 m

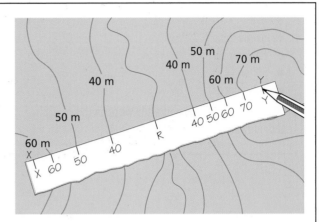

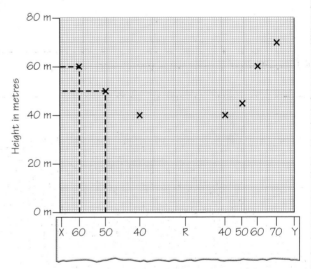

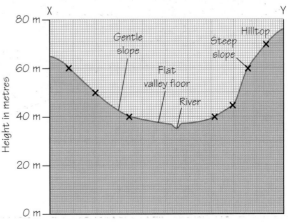

2 Look at Figure 3.2, page 24.

a Draw a cross-section from X-Y. (Turn to Skills Box 6, page 25 to help you.) The horizontal scale on your graph is the distance in centimetres from X-Y. Use a vertical scale of 1 cm = 10 m.

b Label the following features on your cross-section:
- river
- gentle slope
- flat river valley
- hilltop
- steep slope.

c Give your cross-section a title and write on the vertical and horizontal scales.

3 Study Figure 3.4. The bridge crossing the River Portley is very old and has begun to show cracks. Engineers need to build another bridge linking the two settlements of West and East Dinkle. They have decided on two possible locations for the bridge. The two routes across the valley are shown by the dotted lines A-B and C-D.

a Draw two cross-sections to show the proposed routes. Use a vertical scale of 1 cm = 200 m. (A cross section of the current route is shown in Figure 3.5.)

b The bridge would stretch across the valley to join the 700 metre contour line (just as the bridge does in Figure 3.5). Draw the bridges on your two cross-sections. (You can design your bridges as you like.)

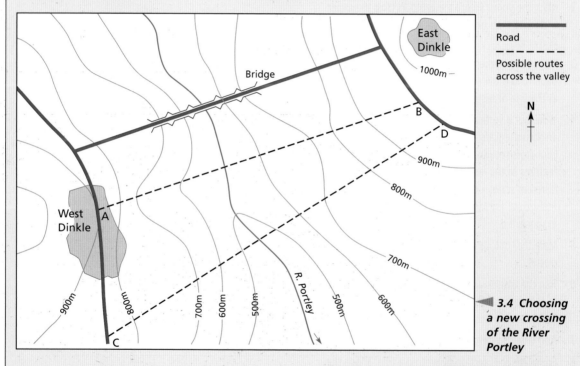

c In deciding which route is best, the engineers are looking for:
- the shortest bridge, as this will be the cheapest to build
- a lack of steep slopes along the link roads to the bridge.

Decide which route you think is better and give reasons for your choice.

3.4 Choosing a new crossing of the River Portley

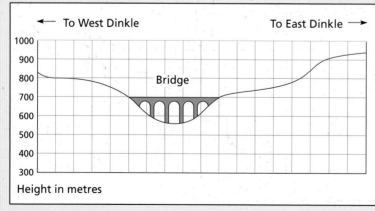

3.5 Cross-section showing the existing bridge over the River Portley

4 Map study: Little Downham (1:25 000)

Find the village of Little Downham (5283) on the 1:50 000 OS map (Figure 2.3, page 15). Now look at the same village on the 1:25 000 OS map in Figure 4.1. Notice how the 1:25 000 shows everything in much more detail.

There are some important similarities and differences between the two maps:

1 The gridlines on both maps have the same values. A **grid reference** for a feature on one map can also be used to locate the same thing on the other map.
2 On both maps, one grid square equals 1 km².
3 The different scales mean that:
 - 1:50 000 → 2 cm on the map = 1 km on the ground
 - 1:25 000 → 4 cm on the map = 1 km on the ground
4 1:25 000 maps have a different key.
5 Some features not shown on a 1:50 000 map are shown on a 1:25 000 map, such as field boundaries.

The best way to get to know the 1:25 000 map is to do some of the activities in this unit.

1 Look at the symbols below. Use the key in Figure 4.2, page 28, to find the meaning of each one.

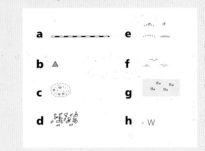

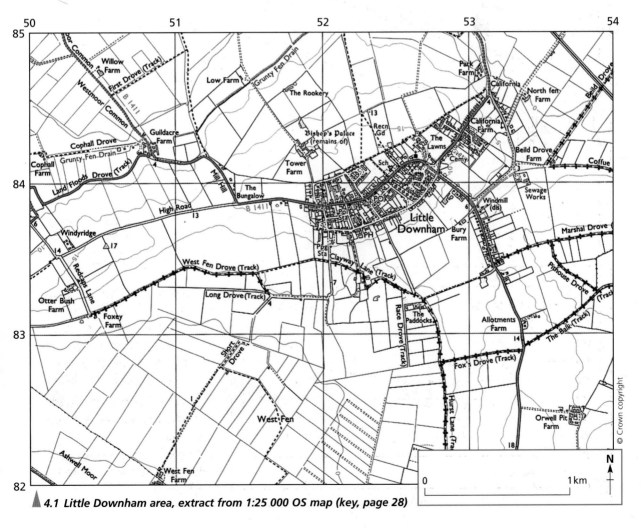

▲ *4.1 Little Downham area, extract from 1:25 000 OS map (key, page 28)*

© Crown copyright

ROADS AND PATHS

M1 or A6(M) — Motorway

A 31(T) — Trunk or Main road ⎫
Secondary road ⎬ Narrow roads with passing places are annotated
B 3074 — ⎭

A 35 — Dual carriageway

Road generally more than 4m wide

Road generally less than 4m wide

Other road, drive or track

⟫⟫⟫ Gradient: 20% (1 in 5) and steeper
14% (1 in 7) to 20% (1 in 5)

Unfenced roads and tracks are shown by pecked lines

.... Path

◆   ◆ National trail or Recreational path

SYMBOLS

Place of worship ⎧ with tower
⎨ with spire, minaret or dome
⎩ without such additions

Building; important building

Glasshouse; youth hostel

Bus or coach station

Lighthouse

Beacon

△ Triangulation pillar

Telephone: public / motoring

pylon pole Electricity transmission line

W, Spr Well, Spring

Site of antiquity

⚔ 1066 Site of battle (with date)

Water

Sand; sand & shingle

National Park or Forest Park Boundary

NT National Trust always open

NTS NTS National Trust for Scotland

Gravel pit

Other pit or quarry

Loose rock

Outcrop

Cliff

Sand pit

Refuse or slag heap

Boulders

Scree

Mud

HEIGHTS

50 · ⎫ Determined ⎧ ground survey
285 · ⎭ by ⎨ air survey

Surface heights are to the nearest metre above mean sea level.

90
75
65
60

Contours are generally at 5 metres vertical interval but on some sheets are at 10 metres vertical interval

RAILWAYS

Multiple track ⎫ Standard gauge
Single track ⎭

Narrow gauge Light Rapid Transit System

Siding

Cutting

Embankment

Tunnel

Road over

Road under

Level crossing

Station

ABBREVIATIONS

CH	Club House
F	Ferry ⎧ Foot
V	⎩ Vehicle
FB	Foot Bridge
MP	Mile Post
MS	Mile Stone
Mon	Monument
PO	Post office
Pol Sta	Police Station (Rural areas only)
PC	Public convenience
PH	Public house
Sch	School
Spr	Spring
TH	Town Hall
Twr	Tower
W	Well

PUBLIC RIGHTS OF WAY

------------- ⎫ Public paths ⎧ Footpath
——————— ⎭ ⎩ Bridleway

+++++ Byway open to all traffic
-·-·-·- Road used as a public path

DANGER AREA Firing and test ranges in the area
Danger! Observe warning notices

BOUNDARIES

— · — · — County (England and Wales), Region or Islands Area (Scotland)

— — — — District

·············· Civil Parish (England), Community (Wales)

VEGETATION

Coniferous trees

Non-coniferous trees

Coppice

Orchard

Scrub

Bracken, heath or rough grassland

Marsh, reeds or saltings.

© Crown copyright

▲ *4.2 Key to 1:25 000 OS map*

2 Write down what you would find at the following grid references on Figure 4.1, page 27:

a 518842 **b** 534840 **c** 525841
d 537825 **e** 526832

3 Make a copy of Table 4.3 to compare the symbols used on 1:50 000 OS maps with those used on 1:25 000 OS maps. Use the keys in Figure 2.4, pages 16 and 17, and Figure 4.2 to help you complete the table.

Feature	1:50 000	1:25 000
Motorway		
Trunk road		
Orchard		
Contours		
Electricity transmission line		
Telephone		

▲ **4.3 Comparing symbols used on 1:50 000 and 1:25 000 OS maps**

4 Study Figure 4.1, page 27:

a Give the four-figure reference for West Fen.

b In which grid square is there a track called Pithouse Drove?

c In which grid square is California?

5 Three crows live in the church with a tower in Little Downham on Figure 4.1. One day they decide to fly to nearby farms to look for scraps of food:
● Crow A flies to Bury Farm (529837)
● Crow B flies to Tower Farm (518842)
● Crow C flies to North fen Farm (534846)

How far does each crow fly?

6 Locate The Paddocks in grid square 5283 on Figure 4.1.

Mary and Alice go on a horse ride from The Paddocks. Follow their route on the map and answer the questions.

The girls turned left out of The Paddocks and headed along Clayway Lane in the direction of Little Downham:

a In which compass direction did they ride along Clayway Lane?

The track took them to the south of Little Downham and headed through grid square 5183 in a westerly direction. It then took them into grid square 5083.

b What is the name of the track in grid square 5183?

c In what compass direction did the girls ride along the track in grid square 5083?

At the end of the track the girls stopped at a farm. They then continued their ride along Redcaps Lane:

d What is the name of the farm where they stopped?

e What is the six-figure grid reference of the farm that they passed on Redcaps Lane?

At the road junction (502835) they turned right and headed towards Little Downham again:

f At what height is the road junction (502835)?

g What is the name of the road along which they travelled?

Joining the B1411, they rode into Little Downham. After passing the police station, but before reaching the Post Office, they turned right and trotted along the road back to The Paddocks:

h Soon after turning right in Little Downham, what did they pass on the left-hand side?

i How far did they ride in total? (Look back at Skills Box 4, page 20, if you need help.)

7 A glider landed in the middle of grid square 5083 on Figure 4.1, next to the triangulation pillar. The pilot of the glider was unsure of where he had landed. Use the map to describe in as much detail as you can what the pilot saw around him as he looked to the north, the east, the south and the west.

8 Look at Figure 4.1.

a Draw a cross-section from the 1 metre spot height at 511826 to Cophall Farm at 501842. (See page 25, for advice on drawing cross-sections.)
● Use a vertical scale of 1 cm = 20 metres
● The 5 metre contour follows West Fen Drove – look carefully at the contours as some of them double-back!

b Locate and label the following:
● West Fen Drove   ● flat land at sea level
● Land Floods Drove   ● High Road   ● hilltop.

Settlement

A settlement is a place where groups of people live. Settlements can range in size from small hamlets and villages to huge cities such as London. Most of the people in the United Kingdom today live in towns and cities.

1 Settlement site

Do you know why and when people first began to settle in the area in which you live? Why did the first group of people settle there and not a few kilometres away?

The ground on which a settlement is built is called its **site**. There are several factors that may have drawn early settlers to a site:

- the availability of *fresh water* from a river or a well

- the need for *fertile* land for farming

- a nearby source of *fuel* for cooking and heating as well as wood for building homes

- the need for land that is easily defended, for example, on top of a hill.

The site of Warkworth, Northumberland

Warkworth is a small town situated on the River Coquet to the north of Newcastle-upon-Tyne. Photo 1.1 is an aerial view of the town. You can see that the town is dominated by its castle. The castle was first built in Norman times in 1150 to fight off raids from the north. Notice that the castle is built on a small hill, adding to its defensive position.

Today the town is visited by many tourists as, in addition to the castle, there are lots of galleries and restaurants along the main street. On the outskirts of Warkworth is a tiny cave carved out of the rock which was occupied by hermits throughout the Middle Ages.

1 Look at Photo 1.1.

a Give two defensive reasons why the Normans sited their castle here.

b Why was it important to be near a river?

c What evidence is there on the photo that the land is good for farming?

d Notice that there are trees in the landscape. In the past there would have been many more. Why would trees have been important to the early settlers?

2 Look carefully at the road crossing the river.

a Describe the two bridges using simple sketches to show how they differ.

b Which one is the new bridge? Give reasons for your answer.

c Why do you think the new bridge was built?

d Do you think it was a good idea to keep the old bridge or should it have been knocked down? Why?

1.1 Aerial view of Warkworth in Northumberland. Notice how the meander of the river seems to wrap around the town

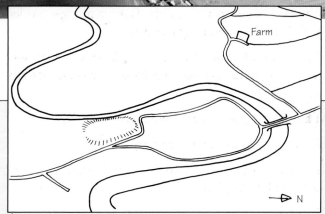

1.2 Sketch map of Warkworth

3 Look carefully at Photo 1.1. Notice that the main road in Warkworth runs down the hill from the castle to the church. The houses along this road are the oldest in the town. In the bottom left-hand corner of the photo are some newer houses.

a What do you think the open space in the middle of the town is used for?

b Why do you think the new houses have been built on the outskirts of the town?

c Notice that the land next to the river is mostly grass. Few houses have been built right up to the water's edge. Try to explain why.

4 Figure 1.2 is the beginnings of a sketch map of Warkworth based on Photo 1.1.

a Make a careful copy of Figure 1.2. Use grid lines to help you if you wish (see Skills Box 5, page 21 if you need help).

b Locate and draw the following features on to your sketch map:
- the castle
- the church
- the area of new houses
- the old bridge across the river
- some of the large fields.

c Label as many features as you can using your answers to the earlier questions. Identify some of the important things (factors) that first attracted settlers to the site.

5 Investigate the reasons for the siting of your home town or village. Locate the oldest part of the settlement and look at a local map to find some reasons why early settlers chose the site.

2 Village study: Little Downham, Cambridgeshire

2.1 The location of Little Downham

Little Downham is a small village in Cambridgeshire. It is located just to the north of Ely (see Figure 2.1). Look back to Figure 2.3 on page 15 to remind you of where it is.

The history of Little Downham

This part of northern Cambridgeshire is called the Fens. It is very flat and low-lying (see Photo 2.2). Much of the Fens used to be under water and so many of the villages, like Little Downham, were sited on hills.

In the Middle Ages, Little Downham became popular with the Bishops of Ely. They built a grand house called the Bishop's Palace, and the village grew in importance. Local farms produced grain, which was sold at Ely market, and a windmill was built to grind the corn. During the 17th and 18th centuries large areas of the Fens were drained to provide new land for farming. Little Downham grew rapidly and many of its people worked in the fields. Today it has a population of about 2000.

2 Use Figures 2.3 and 2.4 opposite and Figure 4.1, page 27, to answer the following questions.

a Give the six-figure grid references for:
- the Bishop's Palace
- Downham Feoffees Primary School
- the Post Office
- the disused windmill in 5383.

b What is the Bishop's Palace used for now?

c What is the name of the road that leads to the recreation ground?

d What are the names of the two pubs on Main Street?

e Use the scale on Figure 4.1 to work out the distance along the road between the church with a tower and The Plough public house.

f What did the firm Chambers do?

g What has happened to some of the land that used to belong to Chambers?

3 Draw a sketch map to show the relief of the Little Downham area. You will need to refer to Figure 4.1 on page 27. Remember to work in pencil first.

a Draw a box the same size as the map extract (16 cm x 12 cm).

Divide it up into the same number of squares as the map extract and write the grid numbers next to the grid lines.

b Now carefully copy the contours on to your map and write the numbers alongside.

c With a light brown colour, lightly shade the land that lies between 10 and 15 metres above sea level.

d With a darker brown, lightly shade the land that is over 15 metres above sea level.

e Mark on the rough area of the village of Little Downham and locate the church with a tower. Mark it with a cross.

f Draw the main road (B1411) on your map.

g The land that you have shaded is a long hill called a **ridge**. Label this feature on your map.

h Complete your map by adding a north point, a scale, and a key and give your map a title.

2.2 Farmland in the Fens

Little Downham today

Nowadays, few people are employed on the land because farm machines have taken the place of most workers. In Little Downham most families own a car, so many villagers commute to work in nearby Ely or Cambridge. They also shop there, in large supermarkets, only using the local village shops for small items. Some modern houses have been built in the village and more are planned. Figure 2.3 shows some of the features of Main Street in Little Downham.

It is interesting to look for signs of change in a village. You can read about a number of changes in Figure 2.4. Even with these changes, Little Downham is a thriving village today, with a strong sense of community.

> **4** Explain why many village shops have closed in recent years. Suggest how these closures might affect the following groups of people who live in villages:
> - the elderly who do not own a car
> - adults who own a car
> - children of your own age.

2.3 Little Downham: Main Street

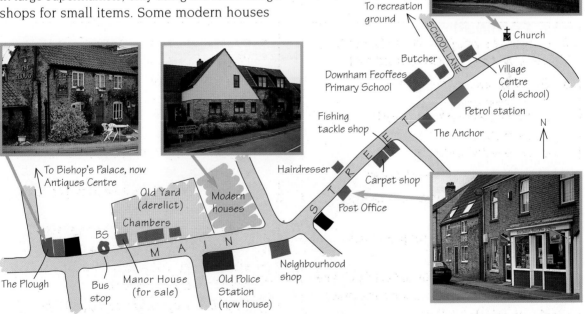

The old schoolhouse has been converted into the Village Centre. Several clubs and societies meet in the hall and it plays an important role in the life of the village.

The police station has closed and the building is now used as a house.

The village library closed. A few books are held in the Post Office for villagers to borrow.

A vegetable packing and haulage firm called Chambers moved to a nearby village, and sold the land for the development of new houses.

2.4 Changes in Little Downham

5 Use your sketch map that you drew for Activity 3 to help you with the following:

a Describe the site of Little Downham.

b Why do you think the village was sited here?

c Can you suggest an alternative place on the map where a village of roughly the same size might have been sited? Show this on your sketch map.

d Where is the B1411 most likely to be flooded? Show this on your sketch map.

6 Carry out your own survey of a local village. You could do the following:

- produce a sketch map, similar to Figure 2.3, to show the main features of the village centre
- make a list of the facilities and services available for people living in the village (e.g. buses, local play groups, local tennis club, etc.)
- look for signs of change in the village (Figure 2.4, on page 33, may give you some ideas about what to look for)
- ask local people about the village (they will be able to tell you about recent changes).

3 A tale of two towns

3.1 The location of Looe and Blaenau Ffestiniog ▶

In this unit we are going to study two contrasting towns – Looe and Blaenau Ffestiniog. Looe is a small fishing port on the south coast of Cornwall, and Blaenau Ffestiniog is a small industrial town in the mountains of North Wales (see Figure 3.1).

Looe, Cornwall

Photo 3.2 is an aerial view of Looe, looking north. Notice how the settlement is split in two by the river. In fact, for many centuries, West Looe and East Looe grew up completely separately. Together they form the present town of Looe.

The history of Looe

In the early Middle Ages Looe was an important naval port. It supplied ships and men for the Hundred Years' War against France (1337–1453). Looe then began to trade with other places. Lime and sand were imported and added to the soil in the fields. This made the soil more fertile for farming. Local granite and copper were exported to Plymouth, Portsmouth and elsewhere. Trading increased and first a canal, and then a railway, were built to link Looe with settlements inland.

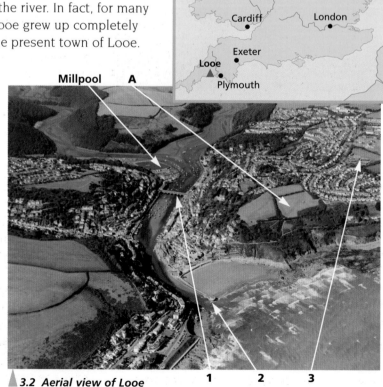

3.2 Aerial view of Looe

Looe today

Looe is an important fishing port. At present there are over 50 boats fishing out of Looe. The main fish caught are cod, sole, mackerel and bass. Crabs, lobsters and shellfish are also caught. There is a fish market on the quayside. It starts at 6.30 a.m. each morning and lasts from one to five hours, depending on how much fish there is to sell. Some of the smaller fishing boats take anglers out to catch big fish.

Today Looe is a colourful and busy town. It still has its fishing industry but it is also a popular tourist centre (see Photo 3.3).

3.3 A typical street in Looe

Blaenau Ffestiniog

The small town of Blaenau Ffestiniog is located in North Wales. It is surrounded by the spectacular mountain scenery of Snowdonia National Park. The roofs, walls and pavements of the town are made from bluish-grey slate that is quarried from the nearby hills. All around the town you can see heaps of discarded slate (see Photo 3.4).

The site of Blaenau Ffestiniog, high on the mountainside, was chosen because of the huge amount of slate there. It is a much younger

3.4 Slate spoil tips around Blaenau Ffestiniog

settlement than Looe. In 1755 there was just a bare cliff of slate above a narrow shelf of poor quality farmland.

The rise of Blaenau Ffestiniog

Slate was quarried on a small scale in the 18th century. However, it was not until the 19th century that the industry took off. The Industrial Revolution increased the need for slate roofing as new houses and factories were built throughout Britain. Much of the slate was taken by railway to the harbour at Porthmadog for export.

The population of the town grew rapidly as more and more slate was quarried. Long terraces of cottages were built to house the workers. Schools, shops, churches and other services soon appeared in the busy town.

The fall of Blaenau Ffestiniog

During the 20th century, the demand for Blaenau Ffestiniog's slate declined. This was because of cheaper slate from other countries and the use of different roofing materials (such as manufactured clay tiles). There are now fewer than 200 people working in the mines. (The town has a population of just over 5000.) Most of the people now work in forestry, farming, local government, tourism or in the factories on a small industrial estate.

A few of the old mines are important tourist attractions. They employ some men who used to work as slate miners. In 1972 the Llechwedd Slate Caverns opened, complete with underground tourist railway and museum. Several craft and souvenir shops, restaurants and cafes have sprung up in the town to cater for the visitors.

However, Blaenau Ffestiniog is still one of the poorest towns in Wales. Many people are unemployed and a large number of the houses in the town need repair and modern-isation. Many young people have moved away from the town in search of work.

1 Compare the towns of Looe and Blaenau Ffestiniog. Make a large copy of Table 3.5. Use the information in this unit to fill in the table.

Characteristic	Looe	Blaenau Ffestiniog
The site		
Origins	12th century (possibly earlier)	
Early activities (functions) of the town		
How were goods transported?		
Population in 1801		
Population in 1901		
Population in 1991		
Present-day activities (functions)		
Description of the town (using the photos)		
Is the town thriving?		

3.5 A comparison between Looe and Blaenau Ffestiniog

2 Draw a graph to show the changes in population for the two towns.

a Make a larger copy of the graph axes in Figure 3.7. Then plot the changes in population of the two towns, using the data in Table 3.6. Use two different colours for the two towns.

Date	Looe	Blaenau Ffestiniog
1801	843	732
1821	1309	1168
1841	1542	3138
1861	1924	4553
1881	2221	11 234
1901	2548	11 433
1921	2868	8138
1941	War – no data available	
1961	3883	6708
1981	4425	5751*
1991	5290	5334

3.6 Population data   *1971 data

b Write the following labels in their correct places. (Be careful to identify which town(s) each label is for.)
● similar populations in 1801
● rapid rise during the Industrial Revolution (1861-1901)
● steady growth during the 19th century
● rapid increase during 1980s
● steady decline after 1901
● similar populations in 1991

c Give your graph a title and make sure that each colour line is explained in a key.

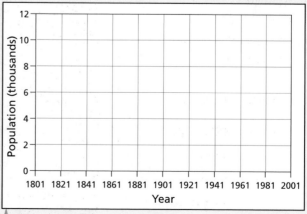

3.7 Axes for population graph

3 As the graph you completed for Activity 2 shows, the populations of Looe and Blaenau Ffestiniog were almost the same in 1801, and again in 1991. Yet, in-between these dates the populations of the two towns differed greatly. Write a few sentences to *explain* the changes in population in the two towns during this period.

4 Blaenau Ffestiniog grew because of local supplies of slate. Looe's growth was partly the result of exporting granite. Find out about slate and granite:
- what are they like
- how are they formed
- what are they used for?

Use encyclopaedias, CD-ROMs, the Internet, and books from your school library. Your school's Science department may have specimens of slate and granite for you to look at.

4 OS map studies: Looe and Blaenau Ffestiniog

Looe map extract

1 Look carefully at Figure 4.1.

a Give the four-figure reference for Pendrym (it is towards the north of the map). In Medieval times, most of the people of Looe lived here (a little inland where it was safe from raiders and pirates).

b Give the six-figure grid reference of St Martin's Church (the church with a tower in Pendrym). It was near here that most of the early houses were built.

c Roughly, how high above sea level is St Martin's church?

d How could freshwater be obtained nearby?

e Why do you think this was a good early site?

Tourist information

◆ ─ ◆ National trail or Recreational path

❗ Walks/Trails

🏛 Museum

☆ Other tourist feature

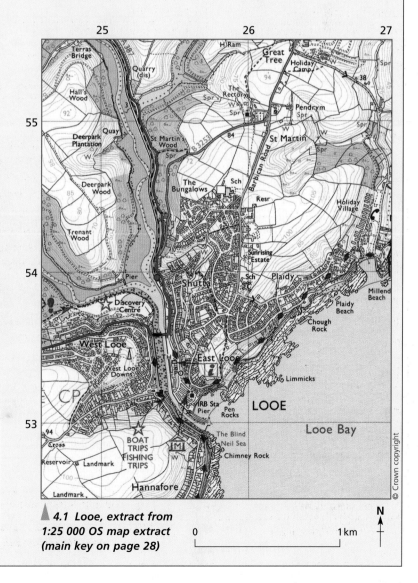

▲ **4.1 Looe, extract from 1:25 000 OS map extract (main key on page 28)**

0   1 km

N

© Crown copyright

2 Look at Figure 4.1, page 37 and Photo 3.2, page 34 to help you with the following questions:

a What is the six-figure grid reference of the Millpool?

b Give the six-figure grid references of the features labelled 1-3 on Photo 3.2.

c Find the Town Hall and give its six-figure grid reference.

d Why do you think the area labelled A on Photo 3.2 has not been developed for housing?

e Roughly, how wide is the sandy beach at East Looe?

f Suggest why the railway and the main road run alongside the river.

3 Why are tourists attracted to Looe?

a Use Figure 4.1 and Photos 3.2 and 3.3, pages 34 and 35, to make a list of the features and facilities that might attract tourists.

b Suggest some possible problems that large numbers of tourists might cause in high summer.

Blaenau Ffestiniog map extract

1 Look carefully at Figure 4.2 and answer these questions:

a Find the spot height in Blaenau Ffestiniog. Give its height and six-figure grid reference.

b What is the highest contour?

c There are lots of contours and they are very close together. What does this tell you about the landscape?

d Blaenau Ffestiniog developed because of its slate. What evidence is there that the area was quarried for slate?

2 What attracts tourists to Blaenau Ffestiniog? Use Figure 4.2, and the information in Unit 3, to make a list of the features and facilities that might attract tourists.

3 In pairs or as a class, discuss what could be done to improve life in Blaenau Ffestiniog for the people who live there. Consider jobs, housing and the landscape.

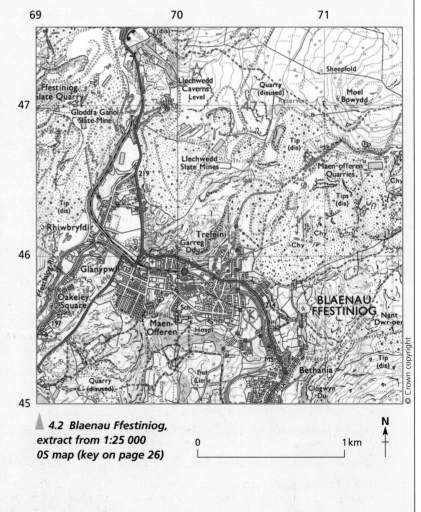

4.2 Blaenau Ffestiniog, extract from 1:25 000 OS map (key on page 26)

0 — 1 km

N

5 City study: Newcastle-upon-Tyne

For hundreds of years, Newcastle has been the regional capital of north east England. It is a very old city, dating back to Roman times, yet today it is a colourful and dynamic centre with modern shopping malls, theatres and universities.

> **1** Look at the photo of Eldon Square in Figure 5.1. Why do you think indoor shopping centres like Eldon Square are so popular?

The history of Newcastle

Look at Figure 5.1 which presents a portrait of Newcastle. It shows some of the well known and important sights and also gives some interesting facts about the city.

Newcastle first developed as a bridging point of the River Tyne. It was a military base during Roman times and it was guarded by a fort. Throughout the Middle Ages, Newcastle grew as a port. Several markets sold wool, fish and farm produce.

A PORTRAIT OF NEWCASTLE-UPON-TYNE

- 80% of Newcastle's employment is in the tertiary sector
- The first electric light bulb was invented in Newcastle

Eldon Square Shopping Centre

- 285 000 people live in Newcastle
- Newcastle is in the county of Tyne and Wear
- People of Newcastle are nicknamed 'Geordies'

- Newcastle has no working coal mines
- Students come from over 40 countries to study here
- 30 000 people take part in the 'Great North Run' every September

- There has been more Japanese investment in the North East than in any other European region
- London is 2 hours and 35 minutes away by train
  Edinburgh is 1 hour and 30 minutes away by train

▲ 5.1

Can you find Bigg Mkt (bigg = barley) and Groat Mkt (groat = oats) on the map in Figure 5.2? Also, during this period, coal became an important export from the area. It was shipped down the east coast of England to London.

Newcastle then became an important centre for heavy industry. It used nearby coal for fuel and, being a port, it was easy to import and export raw materials and goods. Industries such as iron and steel, shipbuilding and chemicals helped the city to expand and to grow in wealth.

Today, many of the heavy industries have closed down. Instead, Newcastle has become a centre for business, health care, entertainment and education.

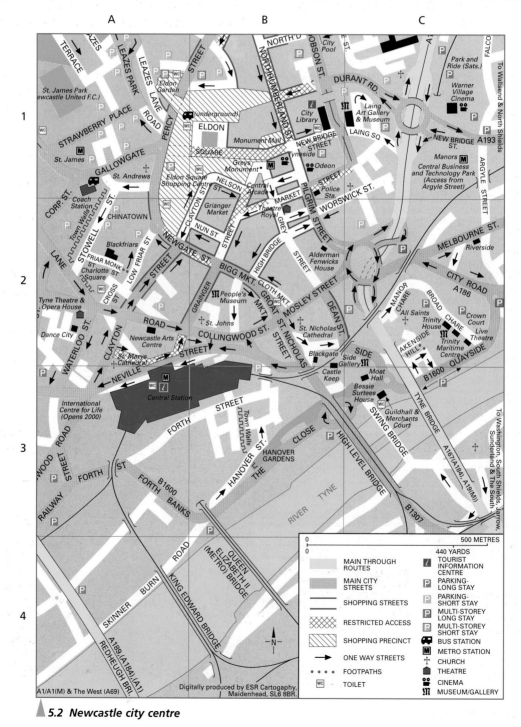

5.2 Newcastle city centre

2 Study Figure 5. 2 and try to answer the following questions. Notice that the grid squares have reference numbers and letters written alongside them.

a In which square is:
- the Tyne Bridge
- Eldon Square
- St James' Park (the home of Newcastle United)
- Chinatown
- Theatre Royal?

b Three street names in grid square B2 suggest that there were important markets in Newcastle many years ago. What did these markets sell?

c Where would you go to find Tourist Information? (Look carefully - there are two places!)

d In which two squares are most of the shopping streets?

e What is the name of the bridge that carries the Metro over the River Tyne?

3 Find the City Library in grid square B1.

a Follow my route and tell me where I end up!

'Walk along New Bridge Street and then turn left into Pilgrim Street. Take the second right into Market Street. Turn left into Grey Street and then first right into High Bridge. At the end of the road, turn left into Groat Market and carry straight on.
What is the tall building on your left, as you enter St Nicholas Street?

b Make up your own journey using the map. Pass your journey to a neighbour to see if they can discover where you are going! The journeys for your class could be 'pooled' so that you can do this activity several times.

Recent developments in Newcastle

1 Shopping

In 1976 part of the run-down city centre was turned into a huge, modern, indoor shopping mall called the Eldon Square Shopping Centre (see Figure 5.1). Over 22 million people visit the centre's 160 shops each year, some from as far away as Norway!

2 Transport

In the 1980s, Newcastle's metro was built (see Figures 5.1 and 5.3). The metro links the city centre with the suburbs and the coast. In 1991, it was

4 Study the map of the Newcastle Metro in Figure 5.3.

a Which colour line(s) would you take if you wanted to travel from Newcastle city centre to:
- South Shields
- South Gosforth
- North Shields
- Wallsend?
- the airport

b Between which two stations can you catch a ferry?

c At which two stations can you change from the Metro to the railway?

d How many stations are there between Wallsend and Whitley Bay?

e What is special about Monument, Heworth, and South Gosforth stations?

f Which stations have car parks?

g Work out the route with the least number of stops from North Shields to the airport. Which lines should you take and where should you change?

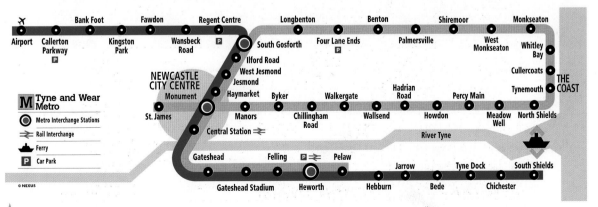

5.3 Newcastle metro

extended to the airport. The Tyne tunnel and a stretch of motorway, running through the town centre (can you spot the motorway on Figure 5.2?), have helped ease traffic congestion.

3 Redevelopment

Empty and run down parts of the old quayside by the River Tyne (see Photo 5.4) have been redeveloped. Some of the old buildings have been restored. They are now used by modern businesses, shops, restaurants and hotels.

---

5 Photo 5.4. shows part of the centre of Newcastle. Find the Tyne Bridge on Figure 5.2. (It is the green bridge with the arch in Photo 5.4.)

a Which way is the photo looking?
(Turn Figure 5.2 round so that you are looking at the bridge from the same direction as the camera.)

b Name the two bridges shown on Photo 5.4 just behind the Tyne Bridge.

c Which of the three bridges carries the railway?

5.4 A view of the Tyne Bridge, Newcastle

---

6 Look carefully at all the information in this unit, including the photos and maps.

a Make a list of the ways in which Newcastle has coped with the problem of traffic congestion.

b Do you think cars should be kept out of city centres? Give reasons for your answer.

7 Find Quayside (see Figure 5.2) on Photo 5.4. Notice that there is a mixture of old, converted buildings and very modern-looking buildings.

a Describe the area on the opposite bank of the River Tyne.

b Either on your own or as a class discuss how this area could be developed. What could be done here and why?

Weather and climate

What is the weather like today? Is it bright and sunny or cold and wet? Is it snowing or baking hot? Most of us are interested in the weather because it affects our daily lives. Warm and sunny weather is ideal for playing outside whereas wet weather often keeps us indoors. How is the weather affecting what you are going to do today?

1 And now, here's the weather ...

▲ *1.1 Flooding in Llandudno, 1993*

On 10 June 1993, the North Wales town of Llandudno was hit by a great storm. The newspapers called it the 'storm of the century'. At least 500 people had to leave their homes (see Photo 1.1). Cars and caravans were swept away as streets were flooded under several metres of water. **Flash floods** followed the heavy thunderstorms, and over 1000 buildings were damaged. The town's hospital had to be evacuated when a torrent of water, more than a metre high, flowed through it.

Storms, similar to the one that hit Llandudno, occur somewhere in the UK almost every year. They are often reported in newspapers and on television. We also hear about strong winds damaging buildings and blowing down trees, snowfalls blocking roads, and ice and fog causing dangerous conditions for drivers. These are a few examples of the more dramatic types of weather that we have in the United Kingdom. Most of the time, the weather is much calmer.

What is the weather?

The weather is the condition of the **atmosphere** (the air above our heads) over a short period of time. It includes the **temperature** of the air, the amount of **sunshine** and **rainfall**, and the **wind speed** and **direction**. Figure 1.2 shows a weather map from a newspaper. Notice how the symbols are quite easy to understand.

1.3 Preparing a weather forecast

1.2 A weather forecast from the Daily Express

The weather is studied by scientists called **meteorologists**. They use radar, satellites and very powerful computers to work out what is happening in the atmosphere above our heads. Photo 1.3 shows John Kettley, a BBC weatherman, studying a satellite photograph. He is preparing a weather forecast. Most forecasts turn out to be correct but, because the atmosphere is so complicated, the weather often changes and the forecast needs to be updated.

Why is the UK's weather so changeable?
The weather in the UK can change a great deal from one day to the next. One day we can be wearing shorts and T-shirts and the next sweaters and coats!

---

1 Read the section 'What is the weather?'

a Explain what the term weather means.

b Make a list of as many different types of weather as you can. Use Figure 1.2 to help you.

2 Write down some of the more dramatic aspects of weather that are reported in the media. Describe the typical problems that occur with each aspect – for example, ice may cause road accidents. Illustrate your account with drawings or cuttings from recent newspapers or magazines.

Much of our weather can be explained by the direction of the wind. The most common wind direction is called the **prevailing wind**. In the UK, the prevailing wind comes from the south-west. This south-westerly wind has travelled across the Atlantic Ocean, before reaching us. As it moves across the ocean it picks up moisture. This is why we have plenty of cloud and rain. South-westerly winds also tend to bring mild conditions because they have passed across the relatively mild Atlantic before reaching us.

In the UK we are affected by winds from several different directions, each bringing particular types of weather. This is why our weather is so changeable. Northerly winds (winds coming from the north) bring cold weather, whereas southerly winds bring warm weather.

3 Study the weather map in Figure 1.2 to answer the questions below. (You may also need to refer to Atlas Maps A and B, pages 9 and 10.)

a Which of the following statements best describes the weather across the UK:
- dry and sunny
- cold with snow showers
- sunny intervals and showers
- cloudy with heavy rain?

b In which areas of the UK is no sunshine forecast?

c What temperature is forecast for north-east Scotland?

d In which part of the UK is the highest temperature forecast?

e What is the temperature?

f Where in Wales is no rain forecast?

g From which direction is the wind blowing in Scotland?

h How does the weather in central and eastern Scotland differ from that in Northern Ireland?

i A friend is travelling from Edinburgh to London. Describe the weather that she will experience on her journey south.

4 For this activity you need an outline map of the UK.

a Use symbols to plot the weather forecast information given in Table 1.4 on your outline map. You could use symbols like those in Figure 1.2 or make up your own.

b Use your forecast to write a few sentences for a radio broadcast. Make your forecast as lively and entertaining as you can but keep to the facts. Read out your forecast to the rest of your class.

5 Read the section 'Why is the UK's weather so changeable?'

a What is meant by the term **prevailing wind direction**?

b What is the prevailing wind direction in the UK?

c How do the prevailing winds affect our weather?

d Why is our weather so changeable?

1.4 Weather forecast for the UK: 1200 hours, June 12th

Place	Conditions
Inverness	sunny intervals, 16°C
Glasgow	sunny intervals, 18°C
Edinburgh	sunshine, 22°C
Belfast	sunny intervals, 20°C
Newcastle	sunshine, 22°C
Manchester	sunshine, 24°C
Norwich	sunny intervals and rain showers, 24°C
London	thunderstorm, 24°C
Birmingham	thunderstorm and sunny intervals, 25°C
Cardiff	heavy rain, 24°C
Southampton	sunny intervals and rain showers, 23°C

2 Summer weather

In the summer most of us look forward to sunny, warm weather – ideal for trips to the seaside (Photo 2.1) or just playing outside. The hottest weather in the UK usually occurs when a southerly air flow from northern Africa brings very hot conditions.

In the summer the sun is very high in the sky. The sun's rays are extremely powerful and, during July and August, air temperatures rise as high as 30°C.

High temperatures and strong sunshine often cause problems. Many people suffer from sunburn and heat stroke if they are in the direct sun without protection. The soil dries out rapidly, and plants and animals suffer. Long dry spells lead to water shortages in parts of the UK. Some places ban the use of hosepipes in order to save water.

2.1 A hot, summer's day

The summer of 1995

The summer of 1995 broke several records. It was the:

- third hottest summer on record
- second driest summer since records began – the driest was in 1800
- hottest and sunniest month of August ever recorded.

While many people enjoyed day after day of sunshine, there were several problems, as Figure 2.2 describes.

2.2 The 1995 heatwave

Scotland
The hot weather attracted swarms of aphids to Scotland.

London
At London Zoo, rhinos Jos and Rosie needed sun cream rubbed on them to stop them from burning.

Peak District
Forest fires raged. Parts of the Peak National Park were closed on the advice of the fire brigade.

East Anglia
Experts warned that millions of ladybirds were about to descend.

Wales
Tap water turned green – Welsh Water had to deliver free bottles of water to people's homes. A spokesman said it was due to the low levels in the Llandegfedd reservoir.

North Devon
300 sheep and 80 cattle were shipped off the Isle of Lundy to Applemore in North Devon, because of a shortage of water on the island.

West Sussex
First hose pipe ban was enforced by Southern Water on 30 June.

---

1 Read the page opposite.

a Why do many people look forward to a hot, sunny and dry summer?

b Study Figure 2.2. List some of the problems that were caused by the 1995 heatwave.

c Suggest other problems that might occur in a heatwave. Add them to your list.

Thunderstorms

An English summer has been described as consisting of 'three fine days and a thunderstorm'. **Thunderstorms** are one of the most dramatic, exciting and yet frightening types of weather that we have in the UK (see Photo 2.3). Every year buildings, trees and sometimes even people get struck by lightning.

▲ *2.3 Why do you see lightning before you hear thunder?*

Thunderstorms usually occur when moist air rises. In summer this is often triggered by the ground becoming very warm. The air in contact with the ground warms and begins to rise – this is called **convection**. As the air rises it cools and **condenses** to form cloud. The rising air forms a towering cloud which often spreads out at the top to form a shape like a blacksmith's anvil (see Figure 2.4).

Strong currents of air develop in the cloud which release **electrical charges**. This is how lightning occurs. The lightning flash causes a sudden heating of the air which causes thunder. Because light travels much faster than sound, we see the lightning before we hear the thunder. Sound travels at a speed of one kilometre in three seconds so it is possible to work out how far away a storm is.

One of the strangest things to see during a thunderstorm is **ball lightning**. Occasionally, after a huge crack of thunder, a ball of light the size of a tennis ball darts around a room or across a garden. Scientists are still not sure how this is caused.

---

2 Make a copy of Figure 2.4 and add the following labels in their correct places:
- towering cloud
- anvil-shaped cloud top
- heavy rain
- lightning
- rising and falling air currents in the cloud.

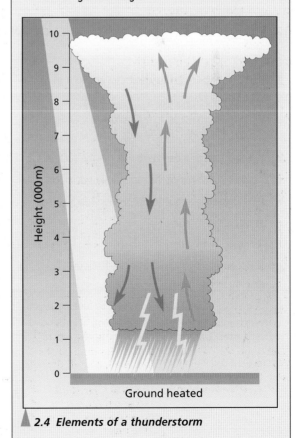

Height (000 m)

Ground heated

▲ *2.4 Elements of a thunderstorm*

TOWNS AWASH AFTER 12CM SUMMER DELUGE

TWELVE CENTIMETRES OF RAIN fell in nine hours bringing chaos to south–west England yesterday. Rivers burst their banks, and householders had to be rescued from their homes.

The downpour in parts of Cornwall was more than twice the average for the whole of June.

An extensive clean-up was under way in Helston, scene of the worst of the deluge. Residents in the lower part of the town had to be evacuated from first-floor windows as waist-high water washed through the streets, damaging dozens of cars and carrying away furniture.

Mr Richard Thomas said his garden wall collapsed under a 'torrent' of water. 'Three parked cars were hit by a tidal wave. They will probably be written off,' he said. 'Then water came up to the letter box level of my house and just poured in.'

In the town's lowest-lying area, water reached the ceilings of some houses, and firemen had to break windows to prevent buildings collapsing.

Thousands of pounds worth of goods from the supermarket floated out of the door on to the High Street.

Teams of engineers were called in to repair faults after power to 5 000 homes was cut.

Elsewhere the heat continued to cause problems. The M4 in west London was shut when concrete joints buckled.

Another wave of thunderstorms from France was moving into the South last night.

▲ 2.5   *(Source: adapted from an article in the Telegraph, 10 June 1993)*

3 Read the section on thunderstorms and look at Figure 2.4 on page 47.

a What causes moist air to rise to form a thunderstorm cloud?

b Why do most thunderstorms occur in the summer?

c Describe the shape of the top of a thunderstorm cloud.

d How high does a thunderstorm cloud reach?

e What causes lightning?

f What causes thunder?

g Why do we hear thunder after we have seen lightning and not before?

h You have just seen some lightning. By looking at your watch you time 12 seconds before you hear the thunder. How far away from you is the storm?

i What is ball lightning?

4 Read the newspaper article in Figure 2.5. Describe the effects of the thunderstorms that hit south-west England.

5 Read the following poem.

Storm
Jagged light, blue and bright
Flashes in the air
Rumble bumble, crash boom
What's going on up there?

The Man in the Moon is having a party
Fireworks burst and fly
As wild drums and dancing feet
Echo through the sky.

by Clyde Watson

Write your own poem about a storm or a hot, dry, sunny summer's day.

3 The climate of the UK

You have already learnt that the weather describes the day-to-day conditions of the atmosphere. The word **climate** is used to describe the average weather of a place over many years. The climate of the UK is described as **temperate**. This means that it is not very hot or very cold, or too wet or too dry. Generally, it is quite wet and mild. However, there are variations within the UK that we will look at now.

Temperature

Study Atlas Map C which shows January temperatures for the UK. Look at the key and notice that the warmest temperatures are found in the south, particularly in the south-west. Notice also that the western coast of the UK is generally warmer than inland. This is due to a warm ocean current called the **North Atlantic Drift**. This current spreads warmer conditions from the tropics all the way up the western side of the UK and beyond to the western side of Norway.

The coldest weather in January is found in Scotland. It is particularly cold over the mountains. This is because air temperature goes down the higher up you are.

Now look at the July temperatures shown on Atlas Map D, page 50. The warmest temperatures are in central and south-east England. These areas often receive very warm air from northern Africa. This warm air does not always reach the north of the UK. Notice how the south coast is the warmest area. It receives a lot of sunshine and that is why it has high average summer temperatures. The coldest areas are again in the north, particularly in the mountains.

Rainfall

Study Atlas Map E, page 51, which gives rainfall data for the UK. The highest rainfall occurs on the western side of the UK, because air has travelled thousands of kilometres over the Atlantic Ocean. When it reaches land the moist air is forced to rise over hills and mountains (see Figure 3.1). This causes the air to cool and **condense**, and rain falls. This is why there is high rainfall over the mountains on the western side.

3.1 Relief rainfall

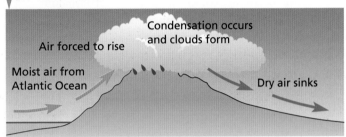

Condensation occurs and clouds form
Air forced to rise
Moist air from Atlantic Ocean
Dry air sinks

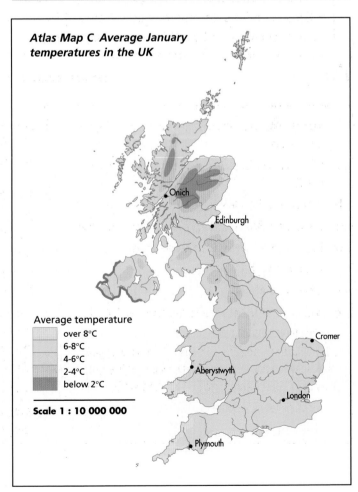

Atlas Map C Average January temperatures in the UK

Onich
Edinburgh
Cromer
Aberystwyth
London
Plymouth

Average temperature
- over 8°C
- 6-8°C
- 4-6°C
- 2-4°C
- below 2°C

Scale 1 : 10 000 000

1 Make a copy of Table 3.2. Use Atlas Maps C, D and E to complete the table.

2 Use your completed Table 3.2 to answer the following:

a Which town has the lowest average annual rainfall?

b Which is the coldest town in both winter and summer?

c Your teacher is thinking of taking you on a school journey to either Plymouth or Cromer. Which resort should be warmer in the summer?

d Describe the differences in climate between London and Onich.

3 Use information in your completed Table 3.2 to answer the following:

a Describe the differences in rainfall between the west coast (Onich, Aberystwyth and Plymouth) and the east coast (Edinburgh, Cromer and London).

b Try to explain why there is such a difference in rainfall between the west and the east. Include a copy of Figure 3.1 in your answer.

	Jan. temp	July temp	Rainfall
London	6-8°C	14-16°C	less than 625 mm
Plymouth			
Aberystwyth			
Edinburgh			
Cromer			
Onich			

▲ **3.2 Average temperature and rainfall in parts of the UK**

4 Use Atlas Map B, page 10, to locate your home town. Now look at Atlas Maps C, D and E and find out the average annual rainfall and the January and July temperatures for your home town.

5 You have been asked to help find a good place for a children's summer camp. Use Atlas Map B, page 10, and Atlas Map D to help you identify those parts of the UK that have summer temperatures above 16°C.

a On an outline map of the UK, shade the areas with average July temperatures of over 16°C.

b Mark three possible places for the camp:
- one must be in south-west England
- one must be in Wales
- one must be in south-east England.

c Write a few sentences to explain why the southern coastal areas tend to be the warmest parts of the UK.

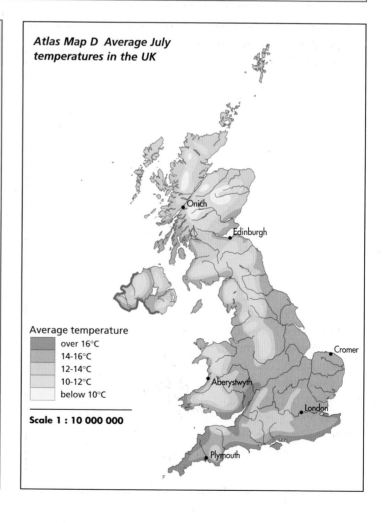

Atlas Map D Average July temperatures in the UK

Average temperature
- over 16°C
- 14-16°C
- 12-14°C
- 10-12°C
- below 10°C

Scale 1 : 10 000 000

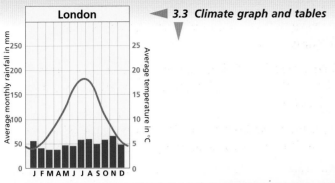

London

3.3 Climate graph and tables

Onich	Jan	Feb	Mar	Apr	May	Jun	Jul	Aug	Sep	Oct	Nov	Dec
Temperature-°C	4	4	6	6	11	13	14	14	12	9	7	5
Rainfall- mm	203	162	127	133	94	125	160	154	190	214	181	236

Cromer	Jan	Feb	Mar	Apr	May	Jun	Jul	Aug	Sep	Oct	Nov	Dec
Temperature-°C	4	4	6	8	11	14	16	16	15	11	7	5
Rainfall- mm	58	46	37	39	48	39	63	56	54	61	64	53

Plymouth	Jan	Feb	Mar	Apr	May	Jun	Jul	Aug	Sep	Oct	Nov	Dec
Temperature-°C	6	6	7	9	12	15	16	16	15	12	9	7
Rainfall- mm	99	74	69	53	63	53	70	77	78	91	113	110

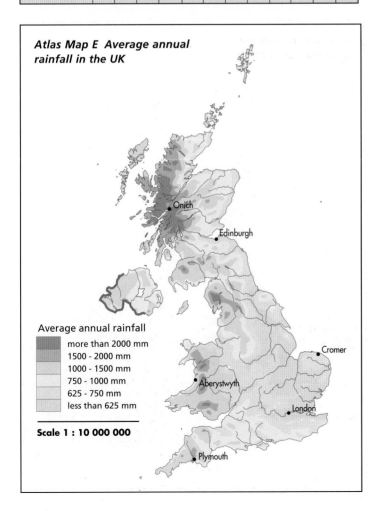

Atlas Map E Average annual rainfall in the UK

Average annual rainfall
- more than 2000 mm
- 1500 - 2000 mm
- 1000 - 1500 mm
- 750 - 1000 mm
- 625 - 750 mm
- less than 625 mm

Scale 1 : 10 000 000

6 Use Atlas Map A, page 9, and Atlas Maps C and D to help you answer the following:

a Which two mountain ranges have the lowest January temperatures? What are the temperatures?

b What are the coldest temperatures found in the Pennines?

c What is the January temperature in the Cambrian mountains?

d Which mountain ranges are the coolest in July? What are the lowest temperatures recorded?

e Locate Dartmoor in south-west England. Does this upland area have temperature and rainfall values that differ from other parts of south-west England?

f Locate an upland area of your choice. (It might be a place you live near or that you have visited.) Use Atlas Maps C, D and E to describe its rainfall and temperature. Compare these values to those of the surrounding area.

7 Most rain falls on the western side of the UK but most people live in the south and east. How might this be a problem for water supply?

8 Look at the climate graph and tables in Figure 3.3. Draw climate graphs for Onich, Cromer and Plymouth, using the figures given in the tables. Use the London graph as a guide.

51

Coasts

The coast is a battleground between the land and the sea. The shape of the coastline is always changing. In some places the sea is eating away at the land forming steep cliffs, yet at other places it is building new land in the form of sandy beaches.

1 Weathering and erosion at the coast

Photo 1.1 shows a cliff on the North Yorkshire coast near Scarborough. At the foot of the cliff you can see some large blocks of rock which have fallen from the cliff-face. Like many cliffs, it is a dangerous place to walk under or play near.

The cliff is being worn away by a combination of two very important, but different, processes: **weathering** and **erosion**. Weathering is the gradual crumbling or decay of the rocks that make up the cliff. Erosion occurs when whole rock fragments are broken off the cliff by the sea. The sea then carries away the rock fragments.

Weathering

The rocks that make up the cliff in Photo 1.1 are being attacked by a number of different types of weathering. One of the most important types involves water freezing and thawing. It is called **frost shattering**. Figure 1.2 explains this process. Frost shattering is most effective when freezing and thawing occurs over and over again.

Another type of weathering is **salt weathering**. This is common at the coast, as seawater contains salt. When seawater soaks into a rock, evaporation may occur, leaving behind crystals of salt. (You may have done an experiment in Science to show how crystals grow.) As the salt crystals grow they

1.1 A cliff on the North Yorkshire coast

52

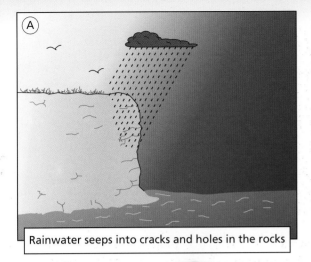

Rainwater seeps into cracks and holes in the rocks

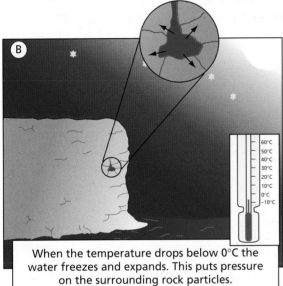

When the temperature drops below 0°C the water freezes and expands. This puts pressure on the surrounding rock particles.

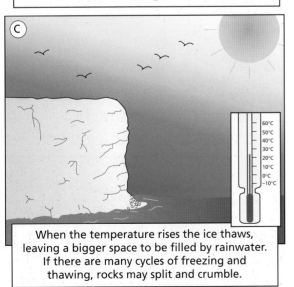

When the temperature rises the ice thaws, leaving a bigger space to be filled by rainwater. If there are many cycles of freezing and thawing, rocks may split and crumble.

1.2 The process of frost shattering

weaken the rock causing it to crumble and break apart.

Rainwater is naturally slightly acidic. The acid in the rainwater often reacts chemically with rock particles. This causes the rock to dissolve or turn into weak clay. The rocks rot and fall apart gradually. This process is called **chemical weathering**.

Plant roots growing in cracks and the burrowing of animals and shellfish can also weaken rocks. This is **biological weathering**.

1 Figure 1.3 is a sketch of the cliff in Photo 1.1.

a Make a careful copy of the sketch.

b Look carefully at the photo and draw the line of the sea on to your sketch.

c Label places on the cliff where there is an overhang. (The rocks here may be the next to fall.)

2 Use the scale on Figure 1.3 to work out the height of the cliff, to the nearest metre.

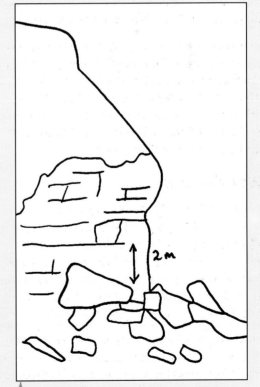

1.3 Sketch of cliff on the North Yorkshire coast

Erosion

The sea is a very powerful agent of erosion. As waves break against a cliff, the sheer force of the water may split the rocks. This type of erosion is called **hydraulic action**. Waves may also hurl loose rocks at the cliff and so erode it further. This is called **abrasion**. Rocks broken by waves are **transported** or carried away by the sea.

From Photo 1.4 it is easy to get an idea of the power of the waves, crashing against the cliffs.

Now look again at the loose slabs of rock at the base of the cliff in Photo 1.1. How and why did they fall from the cliff? First, they would have been weakened by a process of weathering, such as frost shattering. They would then have been undercut by the sea to form an overhang.

1.4 Waves battering a cliff

Eventually there would have been a sudden rockfall to form the pile of rocks that you can see in the photo.

3 Study Photo 1.1. Cliffs can be dangerous places and people should not sit or walk at the base of them. Do you think this is good advice? Give your reasons.

4 Study Figure 1.2.

a Draw one or more diagrams to show how the process of frost shattering works.

b Label your diagram clearly.

5 Look back at the information on weathering and erosion in this unit. Write a couple of sentences to give the meaning of these processes.

6 Copy Figure 1.5 and complete the word puzzle. Use the clues to find the missing words.
   1 Down   A cold type of weathering
   1 Across   A sudden collapse of rocks
   2 Across   It burrows into rocks beneath the sea
   3 Across   Look hard at the sky and you'll spot one on Photo 1.1
   4 Across   Waves hurl rocks at a cliff in this type of erosion
   5 Across   4 Across and hydraulic action are examples of this
   6 Across   A vital part of the process in 1 Down
   7 Across   It's growing on the cliff in Photo 1.1

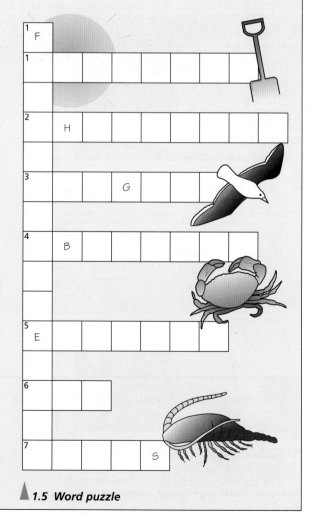

1.5 Word puzzle

2 Coastal erosion: the Green Bridge of Wales

2.1 The Green Bridge of Wales, Pembrokeshire

Greetings from Wales!

BD/IPR/5–11 British Geological Survey

The sea is a very powerful agent of erosion. As it 'eats' into a cliff-line it can produce a number of spectacular **landforms**. The Green Bridge of Wales in Pembrokeshire, South Wales (Photo 2.1), is an example of such a landform. The photo was taken at low tide. The green-stained rock is covered by the sea at high tide.

The Green Bridge of Wales is a landform called an **arch**. It began as a headland jutting out to the sea. The sea eroded it on both sides to form two caves. When further erosion meant that the backs of these caves met, the arch labelled A on Photo 2.1 was formed.

The outcrop of rock, labelled S on the photo, is called a **stack**. There are many of these landforms around the coast of the UK. They are often used by birds as nesting sites. A stack forms when the roof of an arch collapses. You can imagine how the stack in the photo used to be attached to the rest of the headland many years ago.

As a stack erodes, it becomes much smaller. We then call it a **stump**. Stumps are covered by the sea at high tide, whereas stacks are always above

1 The Welsh Tourist Board has asked you to produce a simple booklet for visitors to the Green Bridge of Wales.

- **Your brief:** to describe what there is to see and give a simple explanation of how the landforms developed.

- **Format:** a small booklet or double-sided sheet of paper.

- **Artwork:** include simple sketches to help the visitors spot the main landforms.

- **Layout:** make it neat and interesting.

- **Safety:** tell people to be careful and not to get too close to the edge of the cliff.

- **Further information:** most encyclopaedias, including CD-ROMs, have entries on arches and stacks.

the water. The two rocks, labelled T in the photo, are nearly worn down enough to be covered by water at high tide. Figure 2.2, page 56, shows you how these landforms develop.

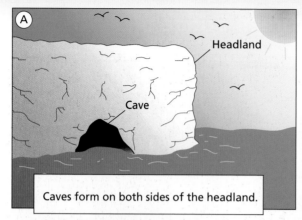

Ⓐ Headland

Cave

Caves form on both sides of the headland.

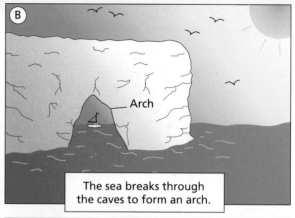

Ⓑ Arch

The sea breaks through the caves to form an arch.

Ⓒ Stack

The roof of the arch collapses to form a stack.

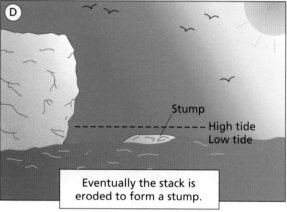

Ⓓ Stump

High tide
Low tide

Eventually the stack is eroded to form a stump.

2.2 The formation of an arch, stack and stump

3 Deposition at the coast

Photo 3.1 shows a typical beach in the UK, probably similar to one that you have visited. There is sand near the sea and shingle further inland. Notice the long, spiky grass on the dunes inland. This is called **marram grass**. It is often found near the coast because it can survive in salty and windy conditions.

3.1 A typical beach in the UK ▶

Where does the beach material come from?

Most sand and shingle comes from weathered and eroded rocks. The rocks are first carried overland by rivers and then **deposited** in the sea. In addition, some rocks come from the erosion of cliffs like those in Photo 2.1 on page 55. Material is also washed on to the beach from offshore sand banks during storms.

How does sand and shingle get on to the beach?

Sand and shingle are washed on to the beach by waves. When a wave breaks it surges up the beach carrying particles of sediment with it – this is called **swash**. When the wave draws back towards the sea, the particles are also dragged back towards the sea. This is called **backwash**.

Waves, such as those in Photo 3.2, often approach a beach at an angle. When this happens, swash and backwash cause pebbles to move in a zigzag course along the beach. This is called **longshore drift**. Look at Figure 3.3 to see how the process works.

Spits – fingers of new land

Longshore drift moves huge amounts of beach material along a coastline. When a coastline changes direction or reaches a river estuary, beach material is often deposited, and a finger of new land is formed. This finger of sand and shingle is called a **spit**. Figure 3.4 shows how a spit forms.

Most spits have a curved tip. This is often the result of waves approaching the coast from a different direction (when the wind changes direction) so forcing the tip of the spit to curve.

3.2 Waves breaking on a beach

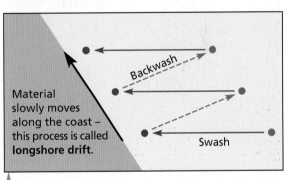

Material slowly moves along the coast – this process is called **longshore drift.**

Backwash

Swash

3.3 The process of longshore drift

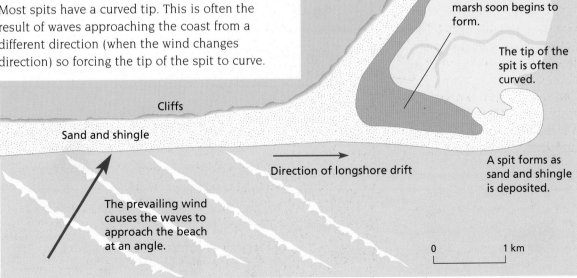

Cliffs

Mud is deposited in the sheltered waters behind the spit. A salt marsh soon begins to form.

The tip of the spit is often curved.

Cliffs

Sand and shingle

Direction of longshore drift

A spit forms as sand and shingle is deposited.

The prevailing wind causes the waves to approach the beach at an angle.

0   1 km

3.4 The formation of a spit

Case Study: Hurst Castle spit, Hampshire

Hurst Castle spit stretches about two kilometres into the Solent to the south-west of Southampton. Look at the map in Figure 3.5 and trace the outline of the spit with your finger. (It is shown by the bold black line that marks the high tide line.) Spits like Hurst Castle are land features and are not covered by water at high tide. Notice also on the map that the tip of the spit is close to the Isle of Wight.

The prevailing winds (the most common winds) are from the south-west. This causes long-shore drift to carry sand and shingle along the coast from west to east. At Milford-on-Sea the coast changes direction, and longshore drift deposits the sand and shingle into the sea to form Hurst Castle spit.

As the spit has grown, the water behind the spit has become sheltered and calm. Mud has been deposited and a saltmarsh has been formed. Can you find the saltmarsh in Figure 3.5 and Photo 3.6?

Look at the map in Figure 3.5 and locate Hurst Castle near the tip of the spit.

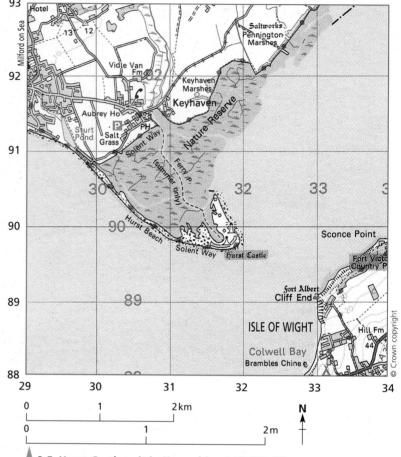

© Crown copyright

3.5 Hurst Castle spit in Hampshire, 1:50 000 OS map extract (full key on pages 16 and 17)

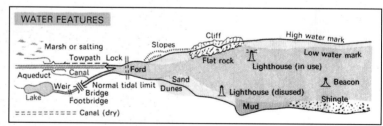

1 Study the map in Figure 3.5.

a Give the four-figure reference for Sturt Pond.

b Give the six-figure references for the following:
- the lighthouse (in use)
- the lighthouse (disused)
- the car park in Keyhaven.

c Is the beach at Solent Way made of sand, shingle, or mud? Draw the symbol used to show this.

d What could you walk along to get from Sturt Pond to Hurst Castle? Draw the symbol used to show this.

e What is the straight line distance from Hurst Castle to Cliff End on the Isle of Wight?

f Suggest why Henry VIII chose to build a castle at this point.

g Measure the distance that the ferry travels from Keyhaven to Hurst Castle. (Look at Skills Box 4, page 20 to remind you how to work out distances.)

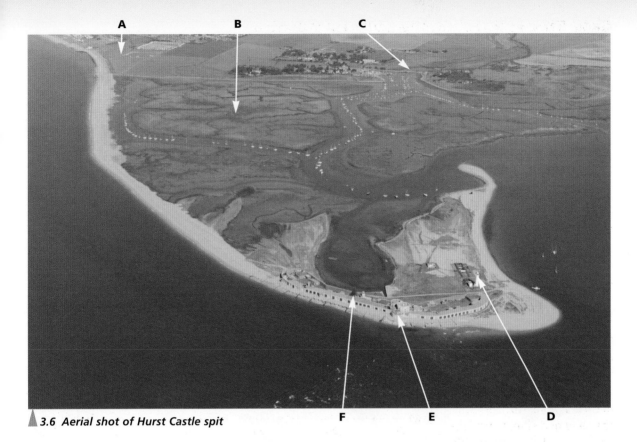

3.6 Aerial shot of Hurst Castle spit

The castle was built by Henry VIII in 1544 as one of a chain of coastal fortresses on the south coast of England. It has been modernised ever since. In the Second World War it was manned with coastal gun batteries and searchlights. Today the castle is managed by English Heritage and it is open to the public.

3.7 Saltmarsh area behind Hurst Castle spit

2 Look at the aerial view of Hurst Castle spit in Photo 3.6. Use the map in Figure 3.5 and the photo to help you answer the following:

a Which way is the photo looking?

b Identify the features A-F on Photo 3.6.

c Was the photo taken at high tide or low tide? Explain your answer.

3 Photo 3.7 is taken from the spit looking north over the saltmarsh.

a Write a couple of sentences describing what the saltmarsh looks like.

b Why are sailing boats moored on this side of the spit?

4 Look at the map in Figure 3.5 and Photos 3.6 and 3.7. What evidence is there to show that this area is popular with tourists? Make a list of your evidence.

5 Follow the steps a–e below to draw a sketch map of Hurst Castle spit. Draw in pencil first and only use colours and ink when you are sure your map is correct.

a Make a copy of Figure 3.8, below. Follow the gridlines to help you draw the outline of the spit. Use a scale of 4 cm x 4 cm = 1 grid square (1 km x 1 km). (Look back to Skills Box 5, page 21, to remind you how to draw sketch maps.)

b Use the map in Figure 3.5 to help you locate and draw the following features:
- Hurst Castle
- the lighthouse (in use)
- Sturt Pond

- the route of the ferry from Keyhaven to Hurst Castle.

c Label the following features on your sketch:
- the spit
- the area of saltmarsh behind the spit
- the two settlements of Milford-on-Sea and Keyhaven.

d Draw several small arrows along the spit to show the direction of longshore drift from north west to south east.

e Give your sketch map a title.

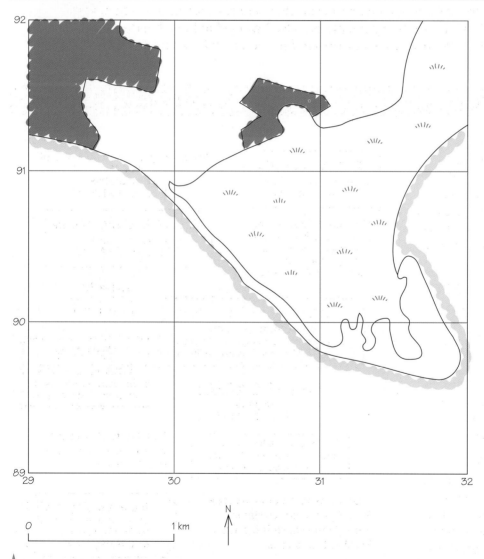

▲ **3.8 Sketch map of Hurst Castle spit**

Industry

Industry is all about the world of work. In the past, large numbers of people worked in smoky factories or on the land as farm labourers. Today, however, most people in the UK are employed in providing services such as education, water supply and health care. Many people are also involved in hi-tech industries, either making electrical goods or carrying out research into new products.

1 The world of work

Figure 1.1 shows some adverts for jobs published in local newspapers. You may have seen similar adverts in your local newspaper. Notice that there are lots of different jobs advertised. The jobs can be arranged into the following groups:

1 **Primary** industries. All industries in this group involve the extraction of a raw material such as in mining, fishing or farming.

2 **Secondary** (manufacturing) industries. These involve making things from raw materials such as cars, computers and cement.

3 **Tertiary** (service) industries. Nowadays many jobs and industries provide a service for people. Banks, estate agents and the Post Office are all examples of tertiary industries.

GRAPE PICKERS
Hard work but well paid.
Would suit students.

Trainee trawlerperson
Enthusiastic, hard working young person needed for general duties on North Sea fishing trawler.

Apple Mac Operators
Immediate vacancies.
A knowlege of QuarkXpress is essential, along with good keyboard skills.

Bertie's Pub Bistro
requires
FULL TIME CHEF

Newquay Holiday Park require reliable CLEANERS for the summer season

Trainee Private Investigator
21–35 years old. Own car with clean licence is essential. Excellent prospects.

Engineering firm in need of skilled:
PLATERS
FABRICATORS
MILLERS AND TUNERS

Holywell Residential Home
has vacancies for two
CARE ASSISTANTS

Dressmaker
urgently needed for fabric shop.

WANTED
BRICKLAYERS
for immediate start on construction sites.

Harts Chartered Accountants
Accountant needed for this small but busy practice.

Golf and Country Club
is looking for an experienced
MARSHALL/RANGER
for its busy golf course

▲ *1.1 A selection of job adverts*

Although most people have jobs, some people are unemployed. Factories close down or companies cut costs by employing fewer staff. People who are unemployed often become poorer. They may need re-training so that they can work in a different type of job.

▼ *Primary, secondary or tertiary jobs?*

◄ 1.2

▲ 1.3

▲ 1.5

◄ 1.4

1 Read the information about industry on pages 61 and 62.

a Draw a table with three columns as shown below.

Primary industries	Secondary industries	Tertiary industries

b Sort the jobs advertised in Figure 1.1 into the three groups. Fill in the table.

c Look at Photos 1.2-1.5. Decide what jobs the people are doing and add them to your table in the correct columns.

d Add another two jobs to each of your columns.

2 Find a copy of your local newspaper - you may get a free one delivered to your home. Look at the job adverts.

a Try to find examples of primary and secondary jobs.

b Cut out some examples of tertiary jobs. Stick them into your book or use them for a classroom wall display. Try to find a variety of job types.

3 Look at Table 1.6 which gives the percentage of people employed in various industries. Figure 1.7 shows some of this information as a bar chart.

a Draw your own bar chart and complete it using the information in Table 1.6. Use different colours to show the male and female bars. Don't forget to label the bars and to give your graph a title.

b Which type of work employs the highest percentage of males?

c Which type of work employs the highest percentage of females?

d Why do you think there is a higher percentage of males employed in manufacturing and construction than females?

e Why do you think there are far more females employed in education, social services and health than males?

	Industry	Male	Female
PRIMARY	Agriculture, forestry, fishing	2.3	0.8
	Mining, quarrying	0.6	0.1
SECONDARY	Manufacturing	25.1	10.8
	Construction	6.5	1.2
TERTIARY	Distribution, hotels, catering, repairs	20.3	24.5
	Transport, storage, communications	8.4	3.2
	Financial and business	16.5	17.0
	Public administration, defence	6.4	6.2
	Education, social services, health	8.7	30.7
	Other	5.2	5.5
	TOTAL	100%	100%

1.6 Employment in the UK, 1995 (%)   (Source: Regional Trends 1996)

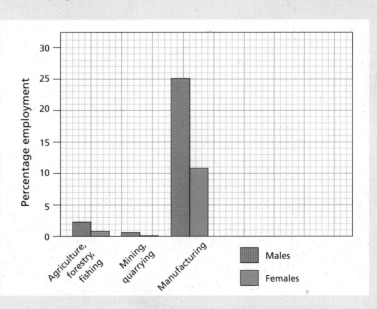

1.7 A bar chart ▶

2 Locating industry

Look at Photo 2.1 which shows a Vauxhall car assembly plant. Notice the following features:

- The assembly plant takes up a large amount of flat land. Can you see the huge car parks used to store the finished Vauxhalls?
- There is a main road (a motorway) very nearby. Parts (called **components**) for the cars are delivered to the plant and the finished cars have to be transported away to be sold. Workers also use the road to get to the plant.
- There is a town in the distance where some of the workers may live.

▲ *2.1 Aerial view of Vauxhall car plant at Ellesmere Port, Liverpool*

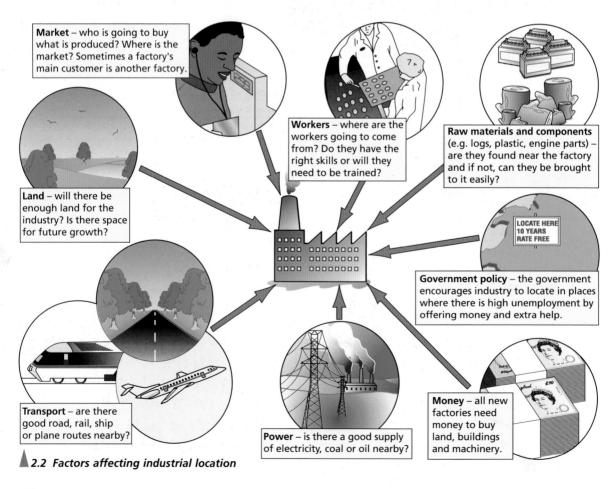

Market – who is going to buy what is produced? Where is the market? Sometimes a factory's main customer is another factory.

Workers – where are the workers going to come from? Do they have the right skills or will they need to be trained?

Raw materials and components (e.g. logs, plastic, engine parts) – are they found near the factory and if not, can they be brought to it easily?

Land – will there be enough land for the industry? Is there space for future growth?

LOCATE HERE 10 YEARS RATE FREE

Government policy – the government encourages industry to locate in places where there is high unemployment by offering money and extra help.

Transport – are there good road, rail, ship or plane routes nearby?

Power – is there a good supply of electricity, coal or oil nearby?

Money – all new factories need money to buy land, buildings and machinery.

▲ *2.2 Factors affecting industrial location*

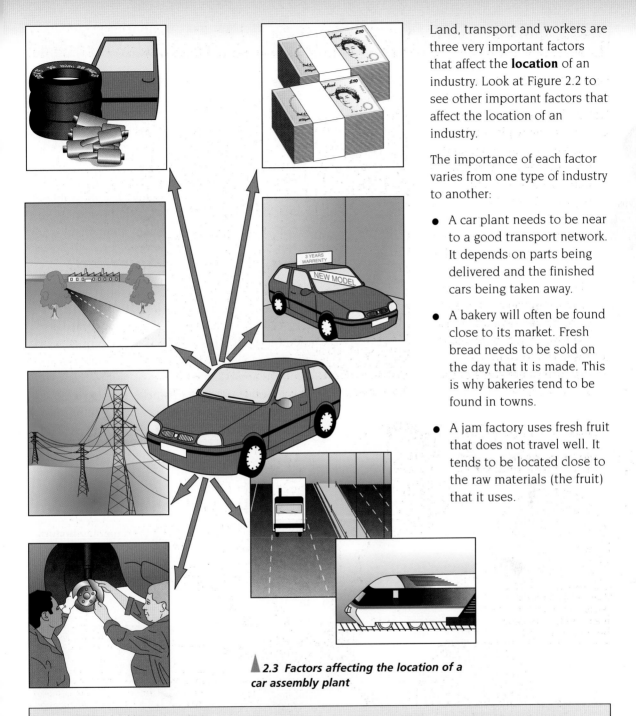

Land, transport and workers are three very important factors that affect the **location** of an industry. Look at Figure 2.2 to see other important factors that affect the location of an industry.

The importance of each factor varies from one type of industry to another:

- A car plant needs to be near to a good transport network. It depends on parts being delivered and the finished cars being taken away.

- A bakery will often be found close to its market. Fresh bread needs to be sold on the day that it is made. This is why bakeries tend to be found in towns.

- A jam factory uses fresh fruit that does not travel well. It tends to be located close to the raw materials (the fruit) that it uses.

▲ **2.3 Factors affecting the location of a car assembly plant**

---

1 Look at Figure 2.3.

a Make a copy of the diagram and write the name of each factor alongside the pictures. Use Figure 2.2 to help you do this.

b Choose any three factors shown in Figure 2.3 and for each one describe why it is an important factor in deciding on a location for a car assembly plant.

2 Which of the factors shown in Figure 2.2 would be most important in locating each of the following? Give reasons for your answers.

a A publishing company that prints local newspapers.

b A factory that makes washing machines.

c A shipbuilding yard.

d A research company producing computer software.

3 Primary industry: quarrying china clay

The open moorland around the town of St Austell, in Cornwall, is described as being a 'moon-like' landscape. Look at Photo 3.1 to see for yourself. The white hills are in fact piles of waste produced by the quarrying of china clay. China clay has been used for hundreds of years to produce a form of china called porcelain. Today, its main use is in paper-making, to improve the quality of the paper.

Only 12 per cent of the china clay quarried in Cornwall is used in the UK. The rest is exported from local ports to countries such as Germany, Finland and Sweden to be used in paper-making.

> **1** Study Photo 3.1. Write a few sentences to describe the scene. Imagine that you are describing it to someone who cannot see the photo. What are your feelings about the landscape?

How was china clay formed?

China clay was formed over 300 million years ago when a rock called granite cooled deep within the Earth. Hot vapours caused part of it to rot and form white powdery clay. Over millions of years the rocks on top of the granite were eroded away and the granite began to show on the surface. Dartmoor and Bodmin Moor in Devon and Cornwall are made of granite.

How is china clay quarried?

China clay is washed out of the granite using a high-powered water jet (see Photo 3.2). The wet clay, called slurry, flows to form a white lake at the bottom of the quarry. It is then pumped to a separating plant. The larger particles of sand are removed and taken by conveyor belt to the waste dump. Some of the finer particles are also removed. The remaining slurry is squeezed in a filter press to remove the water. This produces a more solid china clay 'cake'. The cake is dried and powdered before being transported from the quarry.

China clay and the environment

As Photo 3.1 shows, quarrying china clay results in enormous changes to the natural landscape. It is no longer a natural moorland but a scarred industrial landscape of white waste tips, quarries and lakes.

3.1 China-clay quarrying in Cornwall

3.2 High-powered water jets wash the clay out of the granite

2 The following statements describe the process of china clay quarrying. They are, however, muddled up. Write out the statements in the correct order. Arrange them in the form of a flow diagram if you wish.

- Clay is separated from the larger waste particles of sand.
- China clay powder is transported away to be used in paper-making or porcelain.
- Wet clay, called slurry, flows to form a white lake at the bottom of the quarry.
- Solid china clay 'cake' is then dried.
- China clay is washed out of the granite using a high-powered water jet.
- Slurry is pumped to a separating plant.
- The slurry is squeezed in a filter press to remove the water.
- Sand is removed by conveyor belt to the waste dump.

3 China clay is used by secondary industries to produce a variety of products. Draw a pie chart using the information in Table 3.3. Make up symbols for each segment of the 'pie' to show the products that are made.

Industry	Amount of china clay used (%)
Paper manufacturing	75
Paints and plastics	10
Porcelain-making	10
Medicines, inks and toothpaste	5

▲ *3.3*

4 Re-read the information in this unit.

a Why is china clay quarrying a primary industry?

b What secondary industries use china clay as a raw material?

c Can you think of any tertiary industries that might be linked to the china clay industry?

d Draw a flow diagram to show how china clay links all three types of industry.

4 Secondary industry: making cement

▲ *4.1 Quarrying limestone*

Cement is very important in the construction industry. It is used to hold bricks together when houses are built. Cement mixed with stones makes concrete. Concrete is used for roads and bridges.

How is cement made?

Cement is manufactured from limestone together with shale or clay. These are the **raw materials**. The first stage is quarrying the rocks (see Photo 4.1). Limestone is a very hard rock and it often has to be blasted using explosives. The shale or clay is much softer. It can be extracted using powerful excavators. The quarrying of these raw materials is a good example of a primary industry.

1 Find some examples of how cement and concrete have been used in construction around your school or home area.

67

The rocks are transported to a nearby cement works like the one shown in Photo 4.2. They are crushed and then mixed to form a powder called 'raw meal'. This is then heated to a temperature of 1450°C in a special oven called a kiln. (Coal is burned to heat the kiln.) Chemical reactions take place at this very high temperature and the raw meal turns into 'clinker'.

The clinker cools and then it is crushed to form a powder. A soft white mineral called gypsum is added at this stage. Gypsum slows down the setting of cement (it is also used to make 'Plaster of Paris' and classroom 'chalk'). Finally you get a powder similar in colour to grey cement.

The cement is then stored or packed into bags before being transported away from the cement works (see Photo 4.3).

4.2 A cement works

2 Re-read the information in this unit.

a Why is the making of cement an example of a secondary industry?

b What primary industries supply the cement industry?

c Can you think of any tertiary industries that may be involved with the production and sale of cement?

4.3 Cement ready to be sold

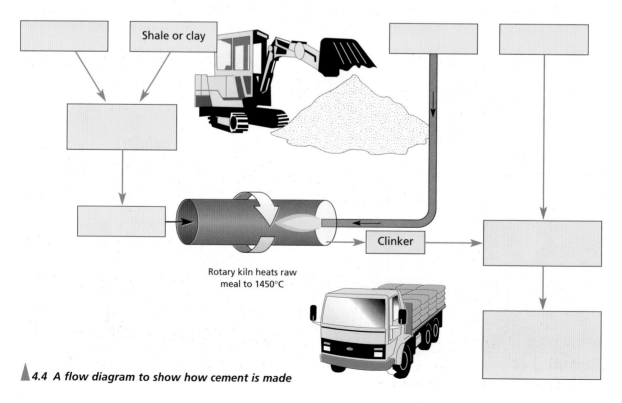

Shale or clay

Clinker

Rotary kiln heats raw meal to 1450°C

4.4 A flow diagram to show how cement is made

3 Look at the flow diagram in Figure 4.4.

a Make a copy of the diagram and complete the boxes by adding the following labels in their correct places:
- Gypsum
- Coal
- Raw meal
- Limestone and shale or clay ground to produce a powder.
- Cement packed into bags or transported in bulk by tankers.
- Limestone
- Clinker crushed to produce cement.

b Use three separate colours to lightly shade:
- the inputs (raw materials)
- the processes
- the output (cement).

Add a key to explain your shading.

4 Look at Figure 4.5 which shows an area in northern England. The quarry is a working limestone quarry that has been supplying a cement works 25 kilometres away. Shale and coal are found nearby. The owners of the cement works want to locate a new works nearer to the quarry and they have identified four possible locations, marked A–D. You have to decide:

a Which location you think is best and why?

b What is wrong with the other locations?

Before you make your decision you should take into account the following:
- limestone is expensive to transport so the cement works needs to be close to the quarry
- there may be some pollution (dust and fumes) from the cement works
- a lot of lorries enter and leave the cement works
- there needs to be quick access to a motorway for the cement to be transported away
- flat land is cheaper to build on than steep land.

▲ *4.5 Choosing a location for a cement works*

5 Tertiary industry: The Post Office

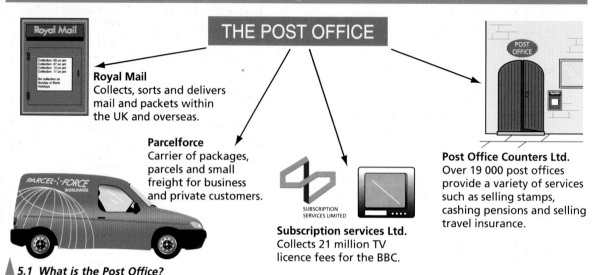

THE POST OFFICE

Royal Mail
Collects, sorts and delivers mail and packets within the UK and overseas.

Parcelforce
Carrier of packages, parcels and small freight for business and private customers.

Subscription services Ltd.
Collects 21 million TV licence fees for the BBC.

Post Office Counters Ltd.
Over 19 000 post offices provide a variety of services such as selling stamps, cashing pensions and selling travel insurance.

▲ **5.1 What is the Post Office?**

The Post Office is a good example of a tertiary industry. It provides us all with a range of important services. It employs over 190 000 people and handles nearly £700 million a year.

What exactly is the Post Office? As Figure 5.1 explains, it is an organisation made up of four separate businesses – the Royal Mail, Parcelforce Worldwide, Post Office Counters Ltd and Subscription Services Ltd.

The Royal Mail

The Post Office started to deliver letters to the public as far back as 1635. Postal services began in London but soon spread to other major cities in the UK. In 1840 a national postage rate of one penny was introduced (twelve 'old' pennies = 5p) and the first stamps were printed (see Figure 5.2). In 1997/8 an incredible 18.4 billion inland letters were posted.

▲ **5.3 A Postbus**

The Royal Mail has its own fleet of 29 000 vehicles. It also uses 400 trains each day and many airline flights to deliver the mail to over 26 million addresses across the UK. In London, the Post Office has its own underground rail system called MailRail.

In parts of the UK the Post Office runs Postbuses (see Photo 5.3) which carry people as well as letters. In remote places these are often the only form of public transport as normal bus services are too expensive to run without extra money from the government. There are now over 220 routes and many people benefit from the service.

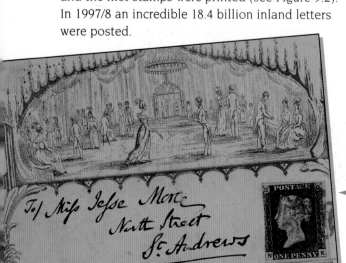

◄ **5.2 A Penny Black – the first national postage stamp**

1 Look at the information in the unit so far, and answer the following questions:

a Name the four separate businesses that form the Post Office.

b How many people work for the Post Office?

c How many inland letters were posted in 1997/8?

d When did the Post Office begin delivering letters?

e How many vehicles does the Royal Mail own?

f What is MailRail and where does it run?

g When was the one penny stamp introduced? (See if you can find out how much a Penny Black is worth nowadays!)

2 Why is the Post Office a good example of a tertiary industry?

3 Study Table 5.4.

a Present this information in the form of a bar graph.

b What does your bar graph show?

c Use your graph to suggest how many inland letters the Royal Mail might be expected to handle in the years 2000 and 2010.

(Source: The Post Office)

5.4 ▶

Total inland letters posted in the UK (billions per year)	
1986/87	12.5
1987/88	13.5
1988/89	13.7
1989/90	14.6
1990/91	15.3
1991/92	15.4
1992/93	15.7
1993/94	15.9
1994/95	16.1
1995/96	17.3
1996/97	17.4
1997/98	18.4

What happens when I post a letter?

Have you ever wondered what happens to your letter after you have posted it? How does it get to the person you have addressed it to? Look at Figure 5.5 and read on to find out what happens.

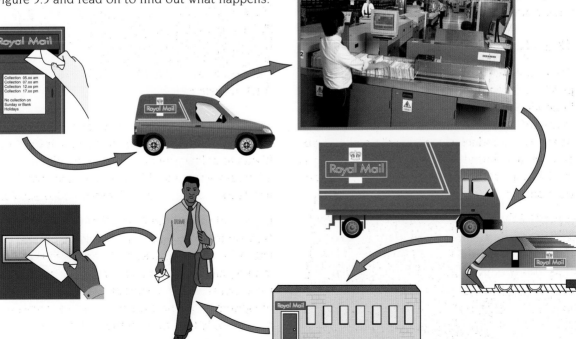

▲ **5.5 From post box to letter box …**

This gives the area that the letter needs to be sent to. The letters (PH) give the main town and the number (4) the district. It is read by a machine in the outward Automated Processing Centre.

This is the local code and is used at the inward Automated Processing Centre to identify the delivery postal round.

Miss Susannah James

9 Croft Street

Perth

PH4 1BX

Each postcode is converted into a special barcode or series of blue dots. (You may not find these markings on every letter.) Each postcode represents a street, part of a street, or even a single address.

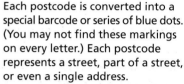

▲ 5.6 Unravelling a postcode

Mail is collected from over 120 000 collection points, mostly the familiar red post boxes. Your letter is taken to the local Automated Processing Centre where it is sorted into first or second class. It is then franked with a postmark.

Now your letter is sorted again. This time the postcode (see Figure 5.6) is used to produce a series of blue dots or a special barcode on the envelope. These markings are read automatically by a machine and your letter is sent off to the right place by road, rail, air or sea.

The next stop for your letter is another Automated Processing Centre near to its destination. Here the postcode is read again to send the letter to a local sorting office. There it is collected by a postman for its final delivery to the person you have addressed it to.

4 Describe what happens to a letter after it has been posted. You could base your diagram on Figure 5.5 but add some written labels to describe what is happening.

5 On an outline map of the UK, mark where letters arriving at your home have been posted. Start by collecting the envelopes that arrive at your home during a week. Then:

a Use Atlas Map B, on page 10, to help you plot where each letter was posted. You'll need to read the postmark on the envelope to do this.

b Draw a coloured line from each point to where you live. (These are called desire lines.)

c Write a couple of sentences describing the pattern that you have drawn. Try to explain the pattern.

6 Make a list of some of the services offered by Post Office Counters Ltd. Work in pairs in class or ask at home for help. You could visit your local Post Office with a friend to find out what services are on offer.

7 In some small villages and remote areas, Post Offices have been forced to close.

a How would this affect local people?

b What is a Postbus and why is it so important to people living in rural areas of the UK?

Environment

The environment is the area where we live. On a local scale, the environment is the area around our home or our school. We might be concerned about litter or noise where we live, or the lack of trees or grass. On a larger scale, the environment is the whole world – all the cities, countryside, forests, seas and the air that we breathe. We might be concerned about water pollution, or the changing climate around the world.

1 Environmental issues

Whether on a local or global scale, one of the greatest environmental concerns is **pollution**. Pollution damages our environment. Most pollution is caused by the actions of people. As Photos 1.1–1.3 show, pollution can take many forms.

1 Look at Photos 1.1–1.3. They show some of the different types of pollution that are common in the UK.

a For each of the photos describe the type of pollution.

b Work in pairs to suggest other forms of pollution which are not shown in the photos.

 1.1

1.2

1.3

Nowadays there is a lot of concern for the environment. You have probably heard of organisations such as Friends of the Earth or Greenpeace. They campaign for protecting the environment. However, as the world's population continues to rise, and people want and expect more and more things, the threats to our environment increase. Here are some environmental issues facing us in the UK today:

- More and more housing is needed. Where should we build? Should more countryside be destroyed to make way for new housing estates?

- Most people want to own a car but cars pollute the air and damage the environment. More cars require new roads to be built, often in the countryside. Should we build more roads? How can we encourage people to make greater use of public transport such as buses and trains?

- The amount of waste and rubbish is increasing. What should we do with it? How can we be persuaded to be less wasteful?

- Chemicals are used by farmers to increase the amount of food produced. But these same chemicals can pollute our rivers. Should this be allowed?

Many people now believe that all future development should be **sustainable**. This means that it should not damage or harm the environment for future generations. Already our environment has been deeply damaged by pollution. We need to stop destroying the world and work hard to protect it. In many countries this may mean that people have to change the way they live. Figure 1.4 describes some ways of living in a sustainable world.

---

2 Describe a recent event that has caused environmental damage. Have a look through newspapers or use the Internet, if you have access to it. You could work as a class to produce a wall display of recent events while you are studying this topic.

---

3 Re-read this page and look at Figure 1.4.

a What is meant by the term sustainable development?

b Use Figure 1.4 to help you suggest how it is possible for us to live in a more sustainable way.

c Do you think the idea of sustainable development is good or bad? Give reasons for your answer.

d Discuss which groups of people might be in favour of sustainable development and which ones might not.

4 Carry out a local environmental study of one of the following areas:
- your own home area (your street, for example)
- your school grounds (as a class)
- the area around your school (as a class).

a To assess the quality of the environment devise your own Environmental Record Sheet and complete it (see Figure 1.5, page 76, for guidance). Add sketches and short written descriptions wherever you can. (If you are studying your home area, choose somewhere that is quite central and typical of the area.)

If you are working as a class, your teacher should select a number of places within the chosen area. You could draw a **choropleth map** to compare the environmental quality of the different places in the area. You could also draw separate maps to compare each of the environmental points that you consider.

b Having completed your study, write a short report, including the following:
1 A brief description of the area that you studied
2 How you conducted your study
3 Any problems that you came across
4 The results of your study (include a copy of your Environmental Record Sheet and any sketches that you made)
5 A brief description of your results
6 Suggestions for ways of improving the environment that you studied.

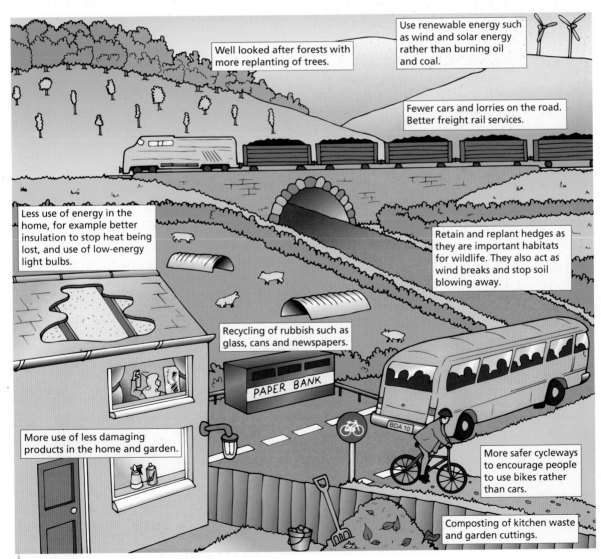

Well looked after forests with more replanting of trees.

Use renewable energy such as wind and solar energy rather than burning oil and coal.

Fewer cars and lorries on the road. Better freight rail services.

Less use of energy in the home, for example better insulation to stop heat being lost, and use of low-energy light bulbs.

Retain and replant hedges as they are important habitats for wildlife. They also act as wind breaks and stop soil blowing away.

Recycling of rubbish such as glass, cans and newspapers.

PAPER BANK

More use of less damaging products in the home and garden.

BDA 10

More safer cycleways to encourage people to use bikes rather than cars.

Composting of kitchen waste and garden cuttings.

▲ *1.4 Living in a sustainable world*

ENVIRONMENT

Complete the record sheet by drawing a circle around a value between 5 and 0 (where 5 is excellent and 0 is poor). Add up all your values and fill in the total score at the end of the sheet.

1 Litter on the ground (look for sweet wrappings, drinks cans, etc.)

No litter   Lots of litter **Value**

5   4   3   2   1   0   ____

Description of litter

....

....

2 State of buildings/gardens (look at paintwork, cracks, etc.)

Attractive   Unattractive

5   4   3   2   1   0   ____

Description of buildings/gardens

....

....

3 State of road/pavement (look for uneven pavement, potholes in the road)

Excellent   Poor

5   4   3   2   1   0   ____

Description of road/pavement

....

....

4 Noise pollution (is it a noisy area?)

Quiet   Noisy

5   4   3   2   1   0   ____

Description of noise pollution (what's causing the noise?)

....

....

5 Overhead wires and cables (look upwards for telephone wires, etc.)

No wires   Lots of wires

5   4   3   2   1   0   ____

6 Traffic flow (how much traffic is there on the road?)

Very busy   No traffic

5   4   3   2   1   0   ____

Description of traffic (cars, lorries, etc.)

....

....

7 'Feel' of the area

Friendly/pleasant   Unfriendly

5   4   3   2   1   0   ____

8 Bright/open   Dull/enclosed

5   4   3   2   1   0   ____

9 Green areas (grass, trees, etc.)

Lot of green areas   No green areas

5   4   3   2   1   0   ____

Description of green areas

....

....

10 Smell (does the air smell fresh or dirty?)

Fresh   Smelly

5   4   3   2   1   0   ____

Description of smell (car exhausts, industry?)

....

....

TOTAL SCORE   **/50**

▲ *1.5 Environmental Record Sheet*

2 What a load of rubbish!

2.2 A landfill site where rubbish is buried

11% Others
3% Textiles (e.g. cloth, wool)
8% Plastics (e.g. bottles, bags)
6% Metal cans
9% Glass bottles and jars
16% Newspapers and magazines
17% Other paper and card
30% Organic waste (e.g. peelings)

2.1 Average contents of a family dustbin

The average household produces 11 kilograms of waste every week. This includes a large range of items such as paper, bottles, plastic packaging, vegetable peelings and nappies (Figure 2.1). The rubbish is collected by dustmen from our homes. Then most of it is dumped in huge holes in the ground called landfill sites (Photo 2.2).

The amount of waste produced increases every year. There are fewer landfill sites available. For these reasons, together with an increasing interest in living in a sustainable way, the government is keen to encourage more **recycling** of materials.

Recycling

Recycling is not a new idea. For years, glass milk bottles and fizzy drink bottles have been recycled. Scrap yards break up old cars for spare parts, and many metals are melted down to be reused by industry.

---

1 Look at the data in Figure 2.1.

a Produce a pie chart to show the average contents of a dustbin. (You will need to convert the percentage values into degrees by multiplying them by 3.6.)

b Suggest which items could be recycled.

> **2** Conduct a study of the waste in your home. You could pool your results as a class.
>
> **a** Have a look at the rubbish in your dustbin. Make a list of the items you've thrown away. Are the proportions similar to those given in Figure 2.1?
>
> **b** What happens to kitchen waste?
>
> **c** Does your family save any of the following:
> - glass bottles
> - cans
> - newspapers
> - plastic containers?
>
> **d** Does your family recycle anything else? Find out if any items are reused. For example, yoghurt pots can be used to grow seeds or store leftover food in the fridge.

Nowadays, people take things such as newspapers, bottles, cans and plastic to be recycled. There are collection points in many places (Photo 2.3). Aluminium cans (drink cans) and glass can be reused by industry. Recycled paper is now found in many paper products including newspapers and writing paper. Maybe the paper that you are writing on has been recycled? Kitchen waste, such as potato peelings, can be turned into compost. It is then added to the soil to improve its quality. Have you got a compost heap or bin at home?

Recycling is a good example of sustainability. By reusing products we help to conserve our resources. For example, by recycling paper we do not have to grow so many trees. Less energy is required to make glass from recycled glass than from the original raw materials. By using compost we do not have to buy expensive artificial fertilisers to improve the quality of our soils.

The Adur Scheme, West Sussex

Adur District Council in West Sussex claims to be the recycling capital of Europe. Indeed, 22 per cent of its domestic waste is now recycled. This is close to the government's target of 25 per cent by the year 2000.

2.4 Blue boxes being collected

All householders are supplied with a blue box in which to put things that can be recycled (Photo 2.4). These items include aluminium and steel cans, plastic bottles and containers, glass containers and newspapers. The blue boxes are put out by the roadside. They are collected by special lorries that have separate sections for the different items.

The boxes are taken to the Materials Recovery Facility at Sompting near Worthing (find Worthing on the location map on page 5). Here, further

2.3 Recycling area at a large supermarket. How could supermarkets play a greater role in helping us to be less wasteful?

2.5 Rubbish being loaded on to a conveyor belt

sorting takes place before the items are collected by the recycling firms (Photos 2.5 and 2.6 were taken at a recyling plant in Otterbourne, Hampshire).

In addition, 8000 householders have been given composting units in which to put organic kitchen waste. Some householders have also agreed to use wormeries (bins with worms in them). The worms eat much of the organic waste (that would otherwise begin to rot and smell) and the dustmen need to collect rubbish less often (see Photo 2.7).

Recycling schemes like the Adur Scheme are expensive to run. The blue boxes, the special lorries

2.7 The inside of a 'wormery'. The worms munch through 2-3 kilograms of waste per week. Liquid compost is drained off using the tap at the base of the bin.

and the sorting, costs far more than the value of the recycled material. However, it does make sense to recycle and it certainly reduces the pressure on our environment. Most people believe that it is a cost worth paying.

2.6 Sorting recyclable materials by hand

3 Read the information in this unit.

a Which four everyday items are most commonly recycled?

b How does recycling help protect valuable resources?

c Use an example to show how recycling can save energy.

d Why do many people have compost heaps or bins in their gardens?

e Draw a flow diagram to describe what happens to recyclable material in Adur District Council. Remember to give it a title.

f What is a wormery and what does it do?

g Do you think recycling should continue even though it often costs more to recycle items than to make new ones? Explain your answer.

4 Discover how good your school is at recycling materials. Work as a class to investigate the following:

● Are there separate bins for empty drink cans in your playground?

● Is waste paper collected to be recycled?

● Is recycled paper used in your school?

● What happens to the kitchen waste? Is it composted, fed to animals or just thrown away?

● Are materials reused in other departments such as Design and Technology, Science or Art?

Present your findings in the form of a brief report. Make some suggestions for increasing the amount of recycling in your school.

5 Produce a poster to encourage recycling. Give reasons for recycling and suggest things that people could do. Use sketches and colour to make your poster interesting and eye-catching.

3 National Parks: conserving the countryside

A National Park is an area of beautiful and often spectacular countryside. It is protected from large-scale development by special laws. Between 1951 and 1957 ten National Parks were established in England and Wales with two particular aims:

- to preserve the natural beauty of the areas

- to encourage their enjoyment by the public.

Recently two other areas, the Norfolk Broads and the New Forest in Hampshire, have been given special protection similar to that of the original ten National Parks. Look at Figure 3.1 to see where these protected areas are located.

The National Parks are very special places. They are not preserved and untouched like items in a museum. Instead, they are living and working environments that change all the time. There are villages and towns in the National Parks as well as industries. Farming is particularly important. However, all developments such as new housing, roads or factories are strictly controlled.

The National Parks are extremely popular with tourists. Several parks are close to major cities and people flock to them when they have free time. They attract a wide range of people including walkers, cyclists, bird watchers and potholers. The many lakes and rivers offer fishing, boating and swimming.

Conserving natural beauty and encouraging large numbers of people to visit can cause conflicts. Traffic jams, litter, noise and gates left open are all serious problems. Recently heavy 4x4 vehicles such as Jeeps have been blamed for eroding parts of the Brecon Beacons and the North York Moors.

1 Produce a map to show the location of the National Parks. Use a large map outline and remember to work in pencil first before using colours and ink.

a Use Figure 3.1 to draw the ten National Parks on to your map outline.

b Add the Broads and the New Forest.

c Use Atlas Map B, page 10, to locate and label the following cities:
- Newcastle-upon-Tyne
- Manchester
- Leeds
- Liverpool
- Sheffield
- Birmingham
- Norwich
- London
- Southampton
- Exeter
- Plymouth
- Cardiff.

2 Find the correct National Park (include The Broads and the New Forest):

a I am located between Manchester and Sheffield.

b I am located close to Southampton.

c I am the only Welsh National Park that does not include a stretch of coastline.

d More people visited me than any other National Park.

e I am the smallest of the original ten National Parks.

3 Study Figure 3.1. Visitor numbers are given for each area. Plot this information in the form of a bar chart. Alternatively, you could plot the bars alongside each of the parks on a map.

4 Study the photos in Figure 3.1 and look at the information in this section.

a Describe in a few sentences the landscapes shown in the photos.

b Which park would you most like to visit? Give reasons for your choice.

c What can visitors do in National Parks?

d Do you think it is right that National Parks are open to the public or should they be closed off?

e Can you suggest any other part of the UK that should become a National Park? Give reasons for your suggestion.

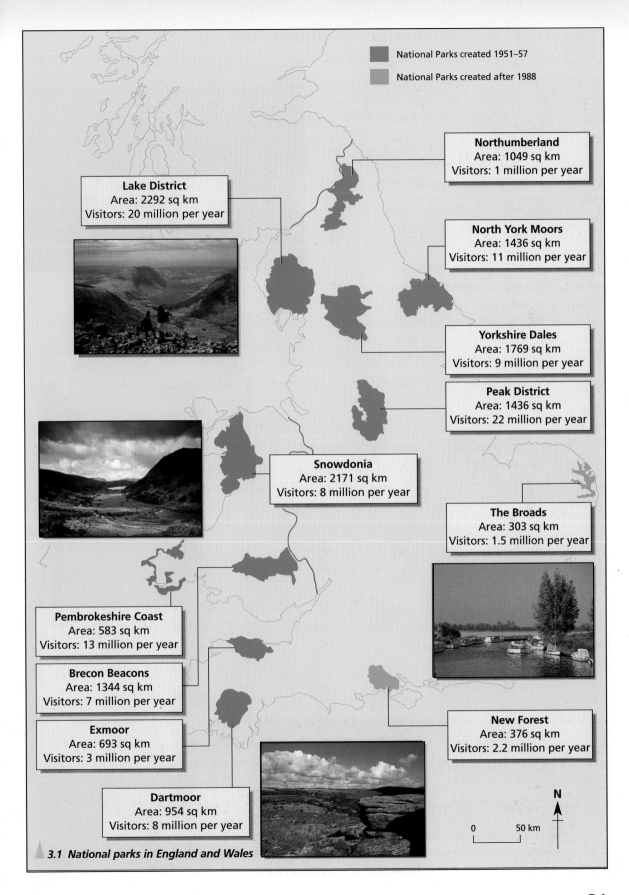

National Parks created 1951–57

National Parks created after 1988

Northumberland
Area: 1049 sq km
Visitors: 1 million per year

Lake District
Area: 2292 sq km
Visitors: 20 million per year

North York Moors
Area: 1436 sq km
Visitors: 11 million per year

Yorkshire Dales
Area: 1769 sq km
Visitors: 9 million per year

Peak District
Area: 1436 sq km
Visitors: 22 million per year

Snowdonia
Area: 2171 sq km
Visitors: 8 million per year

The Broads
Area: 303 sq km
Visitors: 1.5 million per year

Pembrokeshire Coast
Area: 583 sq km
Visitors: 13 million per year

Brecon Beacons
Area: 1344 sq km
Visitors: 7 million per year

Exmoor
Area: 693 sq km
Visitors: 3 million per year

New Forest
Area: 376 sq km
Visitors: 2.2 million per year

Dartmoor
Area: 954 sq km
Visitors: 8 million per year

N

0   50 km

3.1 National parks in England and Wales

Case study: Northumberland National Park

Northumberland National Park (see Figure 3.2) is one of the most remote and wild of the National Parks (see Photo 3.3). The park stretches from Hadrian's Wall in the south to the border with Scotland in the north. It is a working National Park with farming being the main activity. Most of the park is privately owned, but quite a large part is owned by the Ministry of Defence and used for military training.

The National Park is popular with both locals and tourists because there are many things to see and do (see Figure 3.4).

Hadrian's Wall is one of the most famous attractions. It was built by the Roman Emperor Hadrian in AD 128 to form the northern boundary of his Empire. Soldiers guarded it to keep back the 'Barbarians' who lived to the north (in what is

3.3 A moorland scene

now called Scotland). Forts and towers were built along the wall and some of these still remain today for tourists to visit.

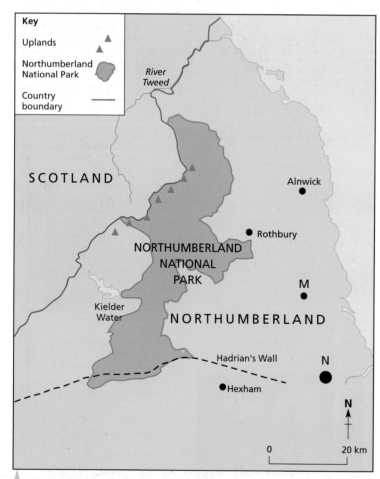

3.2 Northumberland National Park

3.4 Things to do in Northumberland National Park

5 Use pencil first and then colours and ink for this activity:

a Make a copy of Figure 3.2. (Draw a grid over the map if it helps you to make an accurate copy.)

b Use Atlas Maps A and B, pages 9 and 10, to help you identify and label:
- the places marked M and N
- the North Sea
- the upland area.

6 Look at Photo 3.3.

a Describe the photo.

b Which groups of people might like to visit the area shown in the photo?

c Does it appeal to you? Would you like to visit the area? Explain your answer.

7 Table 3.5 shows how the park is made up of different types of land.

Type of land	Percentage of park
Moorland	71
Woods and forest	19
Farmland (mostly used for grazing sheep)	?
	100%

▲ *3.5*

a Make a copy of the table and complete the farmland total.

b Show the figures in the table as a pie chart.

8 The Ministry of Defence owns 20 per cent of the park and Forest Enterprise owns 19 per cent. The rest belongs to private owners such as farmers.

a What percentage do the private owners have?

b Why do you think the Ministry of Defence has chosen to use Northumberland National Park for military training?

c Do you think the park should be used for military training? Explain your answer.

▲ *3.6 Conflicts in the countryside*

9 Study Figure 3.6.

a Make a list of the different problems and conflicts shown in the picture. Can you add any of your own?

b For each one, explain why it is a problem.

c Design a poster, to be displayed in Tourist Information Centres, warning visitors about the problems that they might cause in the countryside. Your poster should encourage people to behave thoughtfully. Use sketches and plenty of colour to make your poster eye-catching. Think of a good title to grab people's attention.

Biogeography

Biogeography is a mixture of biology and geography. It deals with the links between soil, vegetation and living creatures, including ourselves. Biogeography is also concerned with issues such as water pollution and soil erosion.

1 Ecosystems

What is an ecosystem?

Look at the woodland in Photo 1.1. Notice that there are many trees and plants of different shapes and sizes. A number of different animals live in the wood (although they can't be seen in the photo), such as foxes, rabbits and mice. There will also be lots of insects and birds on the ground and in the trees. It is this variety of living things and their relationship with the environment that forms the **woodland ecosystem**.

In an ecosystem there are a number of natural homes where plants and animals live. These are called **habitats**. They include trees, flower beds, hedges and even walls. Each habitat is special and offers just what is needed for the plants and animals to live there.

Nutrients – food for plants!

One of the most important things about an ecosystem is that the various plants and animals are linked together. In a woodland, such as in Photo 1.1, the plants take up **nutrients** (foods) from the soil in order to grow. Animals such as rabbits eat the grass and they in turn may be eaten by foxes. Leaves falling off trees slowly rot on the ground and add nutrients to the soil. Rainwater carries more nutrients to the soil as well as providing the water needed for the plants and animals to live.

▼ *1.1 A woodland ecosystem*

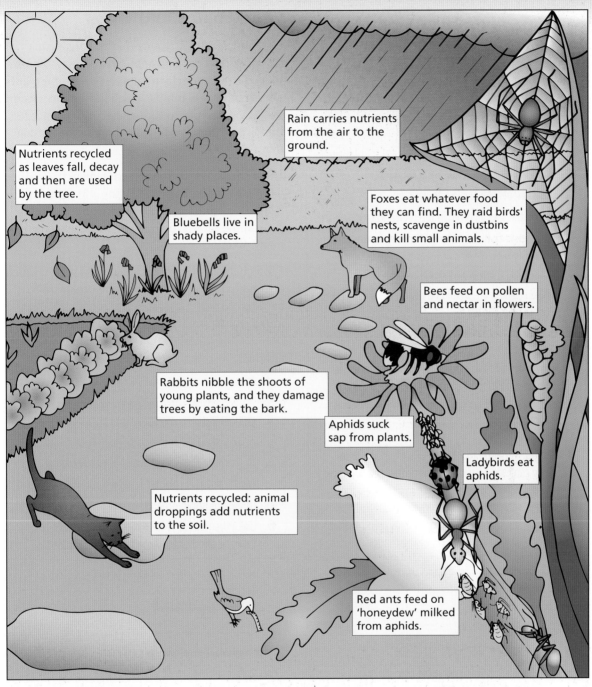

1.2 A garden ecosystem. How many different animals, birds and insects can you spot? Can you think of any others that could be added?

Labels within figure:

Nutrients recycled as leaves fall, decay and then are used by the tree.

Rain carries nutrients from the air to the ground.

Bluebells live in shady places.

Foxes eat whatever food they can find. They raid birds' nests, scavenge in dustbins and kill small animals.

Bees feed on pollen and nectar in flowers.

Rabbits nibble the shoots of young plants, and they damage trees by eating the bark.

Aphids suck sap from plants.

Ladybirds eat aphids.

Nutrients recycled: animal droppings add nutrients to the soil.

Red ants feed on 'honeydew' milked from aphids.

---

1 Draw a sketch of Figure 1.2. Add these extra labels in the correct places:
- Birds eat spiders, caterpillars, snails, and worms.
- Cats eat birds.
- Caterpillars eat leaves.
- The sun provides energy for the plants to grow.
- Spiders suck liquids from bees and flies.

Plants and animals rely on each other and on their environment for survival. One small change, such as chopping down trees or less rain, can lead to major effects on both the ecosystem and on individual habitats. This is why people need to manage natural ecosystems very carefully.

2 Answer the following questions, using your sketch from Activity 1.

a Why is rain an important part of the ecosystem?

b Why is the sun important?

c The shade of the tree is an important habitat for what type of plant?

d How can rabbits damage trees?

e What makes a tasty meal for a ladybird?

f What would the fox like to eat?

g How is the tree involved in the recycling of nutrients?

h Try to identify three different habitats in the garden.

3 Notice that there are no people in Figure 1.2.

a Do you think there should be people on the diagram? Explain your answer.

b In what ways can people affect the garden ecosystem?

4 Now that you have studied two ecosystems, write your own definitions of these terms:
- ecosystem
- habitat.

5 Suggest a change to Figure 1.2 (such as the grass being replaced by paving slabs or the tree being cut down). Discuss how the change might affect the garden ecosystem and the natural habitats. Then write a few sentences, with drawings if you wish, to describe the possible effects of the change.

Food chains and webs

Look at Figure 1.2. Notice that the organisms (living things) eat one another! You may not like this but it is perfectly natural. See how the plants are eaten by the aphids, which in turn are eaten by ladybirds. They in turn make a tasty snack for the birds. Can you see something in the garden that eats birds?

This series of links from one organism to another is called a **food chain** (see Figure 1.3). A more complex diagram called a **food web** (see Figure 1.4) can be drawn to show the links between many different organisms.

Food chains and food webs show the way in which energy (food) is passed from one organism to another. As with ecosystems and habitats, it is important to conserve food chains and food webs because the creatures in them all depend on one another.

6 Study the sketch you completed for Activity 1.

a Draw a food chain similar to the one in Figure 1.3 to illustrate the links between the following:

cat   snail   plants   bird

(these are not in order).

b Use a diagram or write a couple of sentences to describe another food chain shown in Figure 1.2.

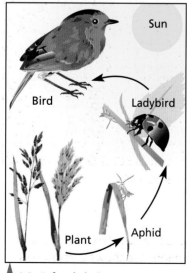

1.3 A food chain

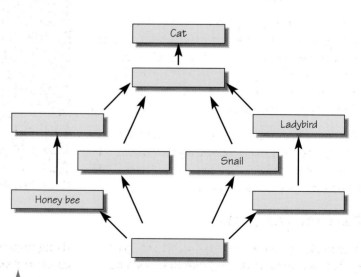

1.4 A food web

7 Make a copy of Figure 1.4 and complete the blank boxes using the following labels:

plants   caterpillar   spider
bird   aphid

8 Write a short account describing why ecosystems, habitats, food chains and food webs need to be conserved and carefully managed. Imagine, for example, what would happen if creatures towards the bottom of a food chain became less common? What happens when forests are cut down?

Make use of examples that you know about or that have been in the news recently. Use pictures, sketches and drawings to illustrate your account. If you have access to a computer with a CD-ROM, you could find information from an encyclopaedia such as *Encarta* or you could access the Internet.

2 Mud, mud, glorious mud!

2.1 *Mud is precious! It can take thousands of years to form.*

▲ 2.2 *Sample of a typical soil*

What is mud?

Photo 2.1 shows some extremely muddy legs! The mud that gets on to your shoes, as you play sport or walk along footpaths, is actually **soil**. It may surprise you to know, as you wash it down the sink, or tread it into the carpet, that it has probably taken thousands of years to form!

Soil is one of the most important resources on Earth. Plants grow in soil and they form the food on which much of life depends. Soil also provides a home for many types of animal.

What makes soil?

Soil is made up of fragments of weathered rock together with organic (living) material, such as rotted leaves and roots. In addition there are living organisms (such as earthworms), as well as air and water. Photo 2.2 shows a sample of common soil.

If you dig a hole into the soil, you will eventually come across solid rock. It is from this rock that the soil develops. The soil that has formed above the rock often has clear layers as Photo 2.3 shows. Each layer is called a **horizon**.

Now look carefully at Figure 2.4 to see how soil is formed.

In Figure 2.4a a bare rock outcrop is gradually broken down by wind, rain and frost. This process is called weathering and it results in a pile of rock fragments.

In Figure 2.4b organic material, such as rotted leaves or plant roots, is then added to the rock fragments. This material is very important because it provides nutrients (food) for plants to grow. It also helps keep moisture in the newly-forming soil.

Earthworms and other burrowing creatures start to live in the soil. They mix up the newly-forming soil just like a kitchen whisk mixes up the ingredients for a cake. Eventually, after thousands of years, a mature soil is formed (Figure 2.4c).

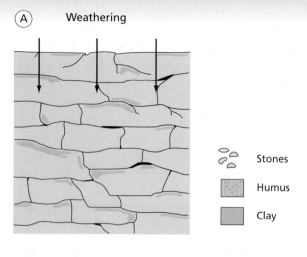

(A) Weathering

Stones

Humus

Clay

(B) **After a few 100 years**

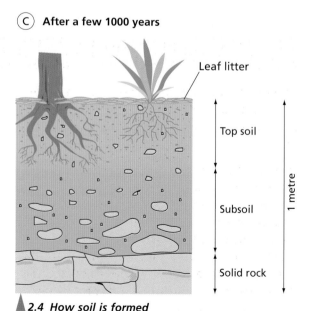

(C) **After a few 1000 years**

Leaf litter

Top soil

Subsoil

Solid rock

1 metre

▲ 2.3 A soil profile

▲ 2.4 How soil is formed

Soil erosion

Whilst soil takes thousands of years to form, it can be destroyed very quickly. When trees are cut down or land is over-grazed by animals, the soil becomes exposed to the wind and the rain (see Photo 2.5). It is then easily blown or washed away. This is **soil erosion** and it is one of the world's greatest environmental problems. So next time you have mud on your shoes, scrape it onto a flower bed rather than washing it down the sink!

▲ *2.5 Soil erosion in high winds*

---

1 Soil is made up of four main components: mineral matter/rock fragments (45%), water (25%), air (25%), and organic matter (5%). Draw a pie chart to show this information. (Remember that to convert percentages into degrees you need to multiply each figure by 3.6.)

2 Obtain a small sample of soil. Let it dry in a warm place. Place the dry soil on a sheet of plain paper. Now draw a simple sketch of your soil sample. Add labels to identify the different components of the soil sample. (If you are unable to obtain your own sample, draw a sketch of the soil sample in Photo 2.2.)

3 Re-read the section 'What makes soil?'.

a Give two reasons why organic material is important in soil.

b What do earthworms do to soil?

4 Make a copy of the diagrams in Figure 2.4. Either add labels or write a few sentences to explain what is happening in each one.

5 Re-read the section on soil erosion.

a What is soil erosion and how is it caused?

b What is happening in Photo 2.5?

c Why is soil erosion a bad thing?

6 Soil erosion is a major global problem. Try to discover more about soil erosion using books, CD-ROMs or the Internet. Discuss as a class some of the ways that soil erosion could be prevented. Try to suggest a solution to the problem shown in Photo 2.5.

---

3 Beinn Eighe Biosphere Reserve

Beinn Eighe (pronounced 'ben-ay') is a mountain in western Scotland. It rises to 972 metres above sea level and it is located about five kilometres south of Loch Maree (see Figure 3.1, page 90).

In 1951 the area between the mountain and the loch became Britain's first National Nature Reserve. In 1976 the United Nations recognised the area as being of international importance. It became known as the Beinn Eighe Biosphere Reserve. (You can see its location on the map on page 5.) Today the area is managed by Scottish Natural Heritage. Its main job is to protect and conserve the natural environment.

What's so special about Beinn Eighe?

Much of the dramatic landscape of highland Scotland was carved by giant glaciers and ice sheets thousands of years ago. When the ice finally retreated (some 8000 years ago) a desolate landscape was left – there were no trees and hardly any soil.

Gradually plants and trees began to grow. After a few hundred years pine woodland covered much of highland Scotland. This type of woodland has now largely disappeared. People have cleared the trees to make way for grazing animals and to provide wood for boat building. One of the last remaining fragments of this original type of woodland is found on the shores of Loch Maree. It is this that makes the Beinn Eighe Biosphere Reserve so special.

Pine woodland contains a mixture of trees including Scots pine (see Photo 3.2), oak and birch. There are many shrubs, herbs and grasses too. They provide natural habitats for a variety of animals. Red deer are common in the area (see Photo 3.3). A few rarer animals such as wildcats and pine martens are spotted from time to time. Falcons and even golden eagles can been seen circling in the sky above Beinn Eighe.

1 Study Figure 3.1.

a Which small settlement lies just to the west of Loch Maree?

b In which direction from Beinn Eighe Biosphere Reserve is the town of Ullapool?

c How far is Beinn Eighe from Kinlochewe (in a straight line)?

d From the car park, in which direction would you walk to get to the Visitor Centre?

e Try to work out the approximate lengths of the woodland trail and the mountain trail. (You may need to look at Skills Box 4, page 20 to remind you how to measure distances.)

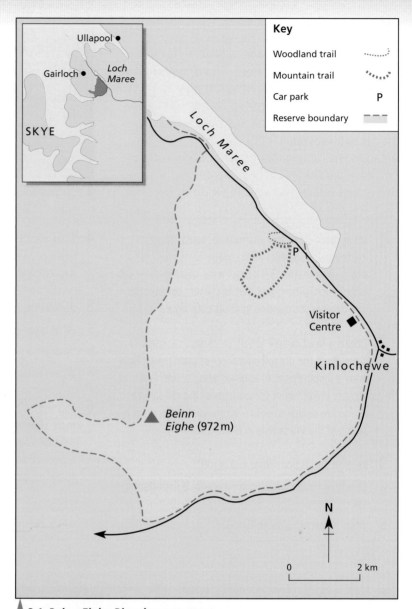

Key

Woodland trail	⋯⋯⋯
Mountain trail	⋯⋯⋯
Car park	P
Reserve boundary	▭ ▭ ▭

Loch Maree

SKYE

Ullapool •

Gairloch • Loch Maree

P

Visitor Centre ◆

Kinlochewe

▲ Beinn Eighe (972 m)

N

0   2 km

▲ *3.1 Beinn Eighe Biosphere reserve*

3.2 A Scots pine ▶

3.3 ▶

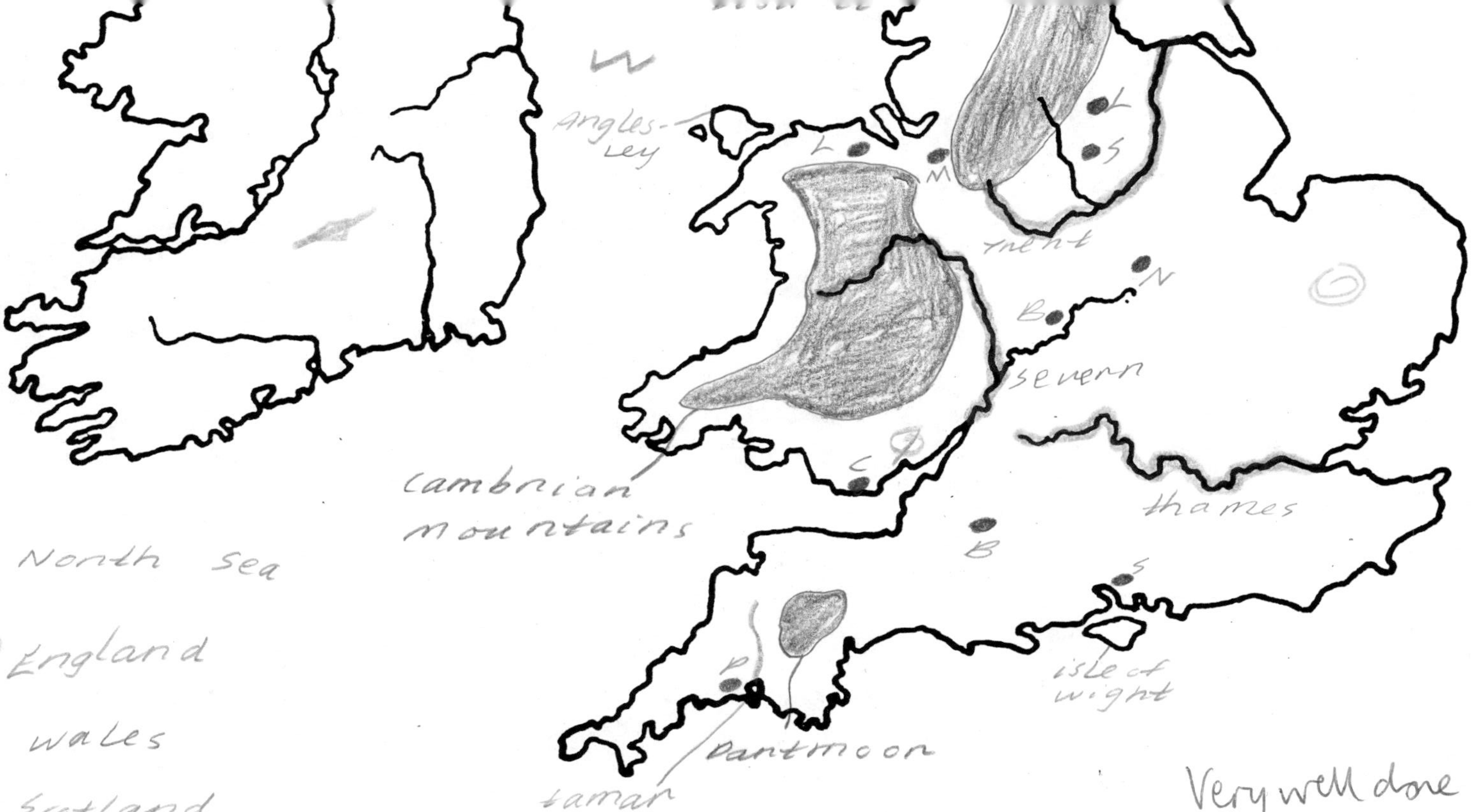

Very well done Jamie. This is really neat and I especially like the key.

Thames

Severn

Trent

Avon

Isle of Wight

Dartmoor

Tamar

Anglesey

Cambrian mountains

North Sea

England

Wales

Scotland

Northern Ireland

Republic of Ireland

The British Isles

Grampian mountains

Southern Uplands

tyne

tees

North west Highlands)

clyde

Legend:
- Mountain areas
- cities
- rivers
- Lough Neagh
- Isle of Man
- Outer Hebrides
- Shetland Islands
- English channel
- Atlantic ocean
- Irish sea

Managing the reserve

Beinn Eighe is carefully managed by wardens from Scottish Natural Heritage. They work to conserve its special environment. Red deer are only allowed to graze in certain places. Visitors are encouraged to use specially created footpath trails. The Visitor Centre at Kinlochewe provides the public with information about the area (see Figure 3.4).

▲ *3.4*

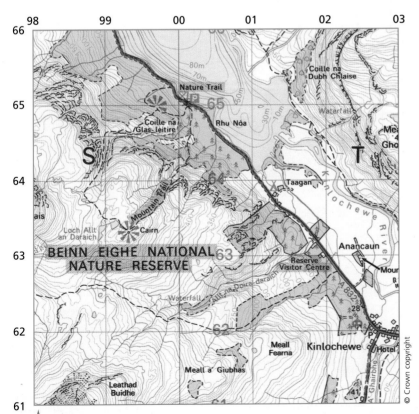

▲ *3.5 Part of Beinn Eighe Nature Reserve, 1:50 000 OS map (2 cm represents 1 km)*

2 Figure 3.5 is a very dramatic map extract. Look at it carefully and work through the list of points below before answering the questions. (You may need to refer to the OS map key in Figure 2.4, pages 16–17.)

- Find the coniferous wood symbols on the shores of Loch Maree. This is the main area of ancient pine woodland.

- Look at how close together the contours are. This tells us that the land is very steep.

- Notice that there are large areas of bare rock outcrops on the mountain sides.

- Find the blue contour lines in the lake. These show the depth of the lake below the surface of the water. Many of the lakes and lochs in Scotland are very deep. They were gouged out by huge glaciers many years ago.

Now answer the questions below and over the page:

a What is the six-figure grid reference of the Reserve Visitor Centre on the outskirts of Kinlochewe?

b What is the six-figure grid reference of the car park at the start of the Nature Trail on the shore of Loch Maree?

c Apart form the Nature Trail what other facility is provided for tourists by the car park?

d What is the greatest depth of Loch Maree on the map extract?

e What is the number of the main road that runs alongside Loch Maree?

f In what way does the landscape change between Kinlochewe and the Nature Trail car park?

g Why might walkers following the Mountain Trail pause for a while in grid square 9963?

h Kinlochewe is a small village but it does have a number of facilities for tourists. Make a list of the facilities available in the village.

i How far is it from the centre of Kinlochewe to:
- the Visitor Centre
- the Nature Trail car park?

j Give a six-figure reference for a bare rock outcrop on the mountainside. Draw the symbol used to show this feature.

k Some of the rivers on the map extract flow down very steep valleys and over waterfalls. Locate a waterfall and give its six-figure grid reference.

3 You have been asked to produce an information leaflet about the Beinn Eighe Biosphere Reserve. It will be available in tourist information offices in Scotland. Your leaflet needs to be single-sided and it should include:
- a simple map of the area showing the two trails and other tourist facilities
- a brief account of why the area is of international importance
- a brief description of the area highlighting its main attractions.

Use the maps and other information in this section. Figure 3.6 shows some typical trees and wildlife found in the area. You may want to include similar illustrations in your leaflet. You could also visit the library to find further material or search for information on a reference CD-ROM or the Internet.

Birch   Scots pine

Golden eagle

Oak

Falcon

Pine marten

Wild cat

▲ **3.6**

4 Enquiry: Peatlands

You may wish to use the information in this Enquiry to produce a longer project on Peatlands or, alternatively, you can work through the activities at the end of each box. The Internet is a good source of information on peat.

ENQUIRY A

What are peatlands?

Peatlands are a very special type of environment. They are found throughout the British Isles. Peatlands have a unique type of soil and form an important habitat for a variety of plants and animals. The peatlands ecosystem is very important but it is under threat.

Some peat facts:

- Peat is the partly decayed remains of plants that have built up over many years in water-logged conditions. It is mostly black in colour. You may have seen peat in bags bought from garden centres.

- Peat forms very slowly – at an average of one centimetre every 10 years.

- Peat forms in waterlogged or poorly-drained areas.

- Peat is important for scientific research. Pollen and plant seeds deep in the peat can tell us how the climate has changed over the centuries. Peat can preserve dead animals and even human beings.

- Peatlands form unique habitats for many plants and animals that are rarely found in other environments.

▲ *4.1 Peat bog in Northumberland National Park*

1 What is peat and under what conditions does it form?

2 Peat in many lowland parts of the UK began to form around 8000 years BC. How thick would such a peat bog be now if had been undisturbed?

3 Describe the landscape shown in Photo 4.1.

4 Why is peat important for scientific research?

ENQUIRY B

Why are peatlands under threat?

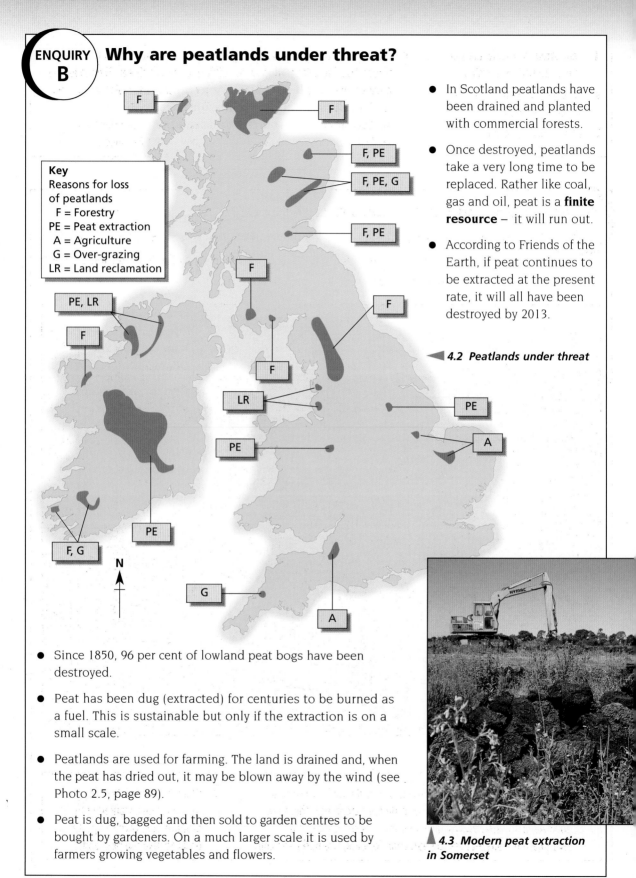

Key
Reasons for loss
of peatlands
F = Forestry
PE = Peat extraction
A = Agriculture
G = Over-grazing
LR = Land reclamation

Map labels: F, F, F, PE, F, PE, G, F, PE, F, F, PE, LR, F, F, LR, PE, PE, A, F, G, PE, G, A

N

- In Scotland peatlands have been drained and planted with commercial forests.

- Once destroyed, peatlands take a very long time to be replaced. Rather like coal, gas and oil, peat is a **finite resource** – it will run out.

- According to Friends of the Earth, if peat continues to be extracted at the present rate, it will all have been destroyed by 2013.

◀ **4.2 Peatlands under threat**

▲ **4.3 Modern peat extraction in Somerset**

- Since 1850, 96 per cent of lowland peat bogs have been destroyed.

- Peat has been dug (extracted) for centuries to be burned as a fuel. This is sustainable but only if the extraction is on a small scale.

- Peatlands are used for farming. The land is drained and, when the peat has dried out, it may be blown away by the wind (see Photo 2.5, page 89).

- Peat is dug, bagged and then sold to garden centres to be bought by gardeners. On a much larger scale it is used by farmers growing vegetables and flowers.

1 Peat often forms a fertile soil and is drained for farming.

a What can happen to the peat when it has dried out?

b Why is this a problem?

2 Make a copy of Figure 4.2 showing the areas of peatland that are under threat. Use five colours to show the different types of threat. Then label the areas of peat listed below. (You may need to refer to Atlas Map A, page 9.)

- The Fens
- Bodmin Moor
- The Pennines
- Northern Scotland
- The Isle of Lewis in the Outer Hebrides
- Central lowlands of the Republic of Ireland.

ENQUIRY C

How can peatlands be conserved?

- Alternative forms of fuel can be used so that peat does not need to be dug up.
- Gardeners can now use peat-substitutes which are widely available in garden centres.
- Old peat workings can be protected and in part restored.

▲ **4.4 Peatland is very fragile**

1 Peat is bought by gardeners because it is a fertile soil in which to grow plants. It can improve the quality of ordinary garden soil. There are, however, many alternatives. Visit your local garden centre and investigate the alternatives to peat. Look for bark, rice husks and coir.

2 What is compost? Should gardeners be encouraged to produce their own compost in order to save the peatlands?

Index

Page numbers in bold denote complete chapter. Entries are in complete word order, rather than in strict alphabetical order.